YOUR HEALTH AND WELCOME TO IT

(A common sense and not-too-serious approach to health issues that we all face)

by

CATHY BRESLIN
&
DR. GARVAN BROWNE

ORIGINAL WRITING

ISBN: 978-1-908024-20-6

A CIP catalogue for this book is available from the National Library.

Published by ORIGINAL WRITING LTD., Dublin, 2011.
Printed by Cahills Printers Limited.

DEDICATIONS

To my mother Mrs. Norah Breslin
For your strength of character, unconditional love,
wisdom and ongoing example
On how to live life with dignity and grace.

In loving memory of my father Mr. Daniel Breslin and
my brother Donal, whose legacy is weaved into the
tapestry of my life.

Cathy

To my mother, Dr. Orla Browne
You have been a rock of support to us all, through good
times and bad.
I think you can look back on it now, and be proud!
We turned out pretty good in the end...

Garvan

ACKNOWLEDGEMENT

We would like to express appreciation to our families, colleagues and friends.

A special thanks to the Breslin and Browne family, for whom we are blessed. Our loving and caring parents, brothers and sisters who are loyal, constant and always supportive. To our nieces and nephews who bring us great joy.

We would especially like to thank Garrett Bonner and Steven Weekes in Original publishing; Peter Occhiogrosso who contributed in the editing of this book; Jim Curtan and Lynn Bell for your help, direction and learning's; and Dr. Carolyn Myss, mentor and teacher, thank you!

Gratitude is extended to all our friends around the world, old and new especially Martin Curry, David Green, Richard Singleton, John O' Leary, Robyn Nijar, Cheryl Rogers, Gina Mc Kie and Rosemary Holton, to mention but a few.

Our special thanks go to those who have touched our lives; teachers, patients, clients and students, all of whom inspired us to write this book.

Thank you Garvan, my best friend, and loyal companion with whom life's journey has become a greater joy.

Thank you Cathy, the centre of my universe and the glue that holds everything together.

And last but not least:

Sincere thanks go to you, our readers.
We hope you find this book helpful, healthful and a practical aid on your life's journey.

Cathy and Garvan

About the authors

Cathy Breslin

Cathy Breslin is a Counsellor, Hypnotherapist and International Author. She has worked and studied in Ireland, UK and USA. She studied extensively with Dr. Richard Bandler, Paul Mc Kenna and medical intuitive Caroline Myss.

Cathy Breslin is one of those rare individuals who combines a deep passion for people with a unique skill set. As well as being one of Ireland's most well known personal development experts, Cathy has a remarkable ability to help people to improve their lives. Cathy maintains that change is possible for everyone at any age and that *"small steps make big changes"*.

Dr. Garvan Browne

Garvan Browne is a medical doctor who qualified in Dublin in 1984. Garvan spent 10 years in the late 1980s and early 1990s, working as a Histopathologist, and Immunopathologist in Ireland, the UK and the USA before returning to Ireland,. He is now a family practitioner in Naas, Co. Kildare. He is an enthusiastic jazz guitarist, and has recently become an aspiring thereminist. Garvan has been drawing cartoons since he was in school, and has had a number published internationally. He is an avid cinema and music fan.

CONTENTS

Introduction 1

Your Health 5

Physical Health 23

Emotional Health 54

Archetypes 78

Relationships 109

Resolve Your Emotions 137

Music 161

Quotes 179

Gratitude 184

Questions & Answers 202

Conclusions 214

Recommended Reading 218

INTRODUCTION
HOW ARE YOU?...

The purpose of this book is to help you make the right lifestyle-choices to remain healthy for as long as possible; to recover from ill health when it happens; and to live with ill health in a positive way when recovery is not possible.

Our aim in this book is to encourage you to examine every aspect of your life, and to realise how everything is connected, and that everything affects everything else. Your emotional health affects your physical and mental health. Equally your physical health affects your mental and emotional health, and finally your mental health affects your physical and emotional health. Change one and you change all.

In general, people do not think about their health, until something goes wrong. As children and teenagers, we think of ourselves as indestructible. We scratch a knee when we fall, or we injure ourselves on the football field, but this always gets better when our mother kisses it (though we don't admit this when we are teenagers). Old people have illnesses, but we will never get old, so we don't have to worry about that.

In the past, people worried more about starvation and war – major calamities, rather than health risks. People expected better performance from their bodies as physical well being was accepted as normal. We have much more leisure time now, but our leisure is much more sedentary.

Why should we think about our health? After all, the whole purpose of being healthy is to allow you think about other things at hand, such as your family, your friends, your work or your hobbies. In times gone past, lifestyles were so much more different than today. Food was simpler – the availability of fruit and vegetables were dependant on the season and the area you lived in.

People's lifestyles were different. There were different working patterns. Women usually stayed at home, once married. Women managed the home, cooking and housekeeping. Children were fed nutritionally balanced and regular meals. Men who were usually the "bread winners" came home to a warm organised house, a piping hot meal, and freshly ironed socks. Roles were more defined. Today, most food is processed, and both partners often work. Meals are rushed, quickly prepared, and convenience is prized higher than nutritional value. Demarcation in social roles is much less clear. Things were not necessarily worse or better then. Our lives have improved immeasurably, but there are things that we can learn from the past.

Although it may not have been the case in every home, many homes provided an environment where one could unwind on arriving back in the evening. Entertainment was controlled, and often censored. One read a book, listened to the wireless, or ventured out to the cinema. The Hayes code ensured that what you were exposed to on the silver screen, would not be in anyway scandalous. Everyone slept in single beds.

There are more diseases in the world, and our immune systems are probably not as strong as they used to be. The population has moved from predominantly rural to predominantly urban and suburban.

The familial structure has changed dramatically over the years. The local extended family has almost completely disappeared. Family breakdowns and break-ups are more common, and more accepted now. The support offered by a large extended family, is no longer available. There is more reliance on government and private organisations needed to maintain normal family development. Families no longer develop naturally, but instead rely on external help to function.

Many people think they are healthy, but are in fact rapidly becoming unhealthy, due to their life choices. There are many years between the unhealthy behaviour, and the consequences to our health. The twenty year old sees no harm in his drinking habits, but will become the forty year old attending AA meetings. Many parents believe that introducing alcohol in small amounts to their children will help them develop a healthy attitude to alcohol as adults. On the other hand, children who start to drink heavily at a young age, develop health problems much earlier. The thirteen year old who goes on the odd fad diet to maintain the latest fashion or celebrity trend, can end up sitting in their doctors office 20 years later, discussing their obesity, blood pressure, heart disease or adult onset diabetes mellitus

We know a lot more now about health risks. For example, we understand now the multiple risks attached to smoking tobacco, which at one point was considered relaxing and "cool". We used to consider alcoholism in terms of sad men in gutters drinking methylated spirits out of a brown paper bag, or a mascara smudged middle aged barfly. Now we understand that what we used to consider "normal" drinking patterns can very easily lead to dependence – for example the cocktail before dinner, or the gin and tonic after work.

Of course having sugary breakfasts, and fast food lunches in your early years is likely to lead to early dental problems (and large dental bills), brittle bones (osteoporosis), and the concentration abilities of a goldfish.

Often the state of their health tomorrow is a direct consequence of their actions today.

"Health is a state of complete physical, mental and social well-being, and not merely the absence of disease or infirmity". - World Health Organization, 1948

This book consists of case histories, interesting facts, anecdotes, down-to-earth no-nonsense advice and a combination of tasks and exercises designed to enhance and direct curiosity, comprehension and change. This is combined with a certain amount of humour to try and distract you from being too serious...
 It is important to perform the tasks as you read the book, as this will help you to both understand the points in each chapter, and also how these apply to yourself.

This book is about your health (and welcome to it..)

YOUR HEALTH
...NOT SO GOOD, THANK YOU

Case History:

Sandy is an important attorney. She is a high powered partner in an expensive legal firm. She works about 14 hours a day, and usually eats at her desk if she is not dealing with clients over lunch. Typically Sandy will grab a super burrito with extra sour cream and guacamole from Enrique's Happy Tex Mex stand in Central Park. She will wash this down with a decaf super soda followed by a double decaf latte from the coffee shop on the corner, to go. Of course she also has the coffeepot back at the office on the go all day (and that is NOT decaf).

When asked why she would eat such a high calorie content meal her reply was that she didn't have time to go to a restaurant for a "proper" meal, and that she wasn't going to get home until late that evening due to her heavy work load. She had an important case in the morning, and had to prepare her brief. She needed the energy boost to sustain her for the rest of the day. She is too busy and under pressure to prepare a sandwich at home... Sandy does not realise that this is not a once off situation. This is a regular occurrence for Sandy. She eats her lunch as she walks back to the office, phone to the ear. As she juggles her brain in reply to important business on her phone, she devours her burrito quickly and ends up throwing the last nutritious bit away because for some reason she lost her appetite. With that she feels irritated and concerned, going over that last conversation with her boss prior to lunch; asking herself mindless questions like did I... was I... where did I put that photo copy... And finally saying "I feel so fat... Hi ho, hi ho it's off to work I go"

At 2:30pm Sandy is feeling drained. At least, she realises, she still has the latte to cheer herself up with when she gets back to the office. As she enters the office building she says to herself "what the hey, I'll have a quick smoke before I go in, after all that could help me relax" (good thinking Sandy).

She puffs her cigarette as if it was her last and then throws her head back, with a smile on her face, albeit strained and put on. She returns to her office, sips on her latte and glances at her family photo on her desk. She suddenly realises that her daughter Jamie, who has just turned 13 years of age, is giving a violin recital at her school. Sandy had promised her that she would be there – darn it, how could she forget. She tries desperately to contact her ex-husband to ask him if he could go there instead of her. His phone is out of coverage. What will sandy do? Meanwhile her office phone is lighting up with incoming calls one of which is a conference call with her sister company in the UK. Her internal dialog goes something like - Darn, oh no, where is that file?

When she gets home that night, she indulges in a stiff Martini which helps her to unwind… Her daughter is very disappointed that she did not come to her recital, and mutters to herself as she goes up the stairs, "What's new"…

JAMIE

What is Sandy's potential future?

Bad Scenario: Sandy's lifestyle: Sandy is stressed. Sandy is eating short-term energy boosting food. This is a short-term solution to potentially long-term health problems.

Her problems could be more serious than a bad diet

- Premature ageing and early death
- Obesity
- High blood cholesterol level and coronary heart disease
- Diabetes
- Bowel disease
- Blood vessel disease
- Depression
- Low sex drive
- Relationship problems
- Low energy and lack of enthusiasm
- A life long addiction to fast food
- A daughter who plays with the New York Symphony Orchestra, but does not talk to her Mom...

Good Scenario: Sandy changes her lifestyle. Sandy is relaxed. She makes her healthy lunch at home and takes it to the office with her. She takes time for herself and for some gentle exercise. She has a healthier work/home balance. Her future health prospects are likely to be:

- Steady weight and a high level of fitness
- Healthy heart and a low blood cholesterol level
- Healthy digestive system
- High energy levels
- Happier outlook on life
- Positive relationships
- Healthy sex life
- Rare encounters with fast food
- A daughter who plays with the New York Symphony Orchestra, and is managed by her Mom...

So where is Sandy now, and what are the priorities in her life?

Sandy is at a crossroads without a map yet. Her priorities are her work and career. She is focusing on making ends meet. She is giving little time to herself, or her family. While she thinks that she is securing her future and that of her family, she actually rarely thinks beyond the short term and the next problem that she is facing.

Sandy is not having a "bad hair day". Sandy is experiencing a typical day in her work life. She is 33 going on 53. As Sandy is focusing on the financial needs of her family, and of the Company that she works for, she, in fact, may be quite unaware of her own needs. If asked, she might just say that she is on a treadmill. She just "does". She doesn't have the time to spend thinking of herself, or worrying about "silly things" like stress, proper nutrition or exercise.

Sandy wonders. What can she do to improve things?

As she descends, the following morning, from her en-suite bathroom and gazes at her once slender and toned physique she falls into a slight depression. The front door slams as her daughter leaves for school without even a "see you later mom". She looks around her house and notices the accumulated dust in disbelief. The once trendy and fashionable furniture is rapidly becoming old and tatty. She sits on her bed and says to herself "This just can't go on… What has my world turned into?" It is time to take inventory of her life.

Sandy decides to take a day off for herself. She goes for a walk in a local park with a pen and notepad in hand. She sits on a park bench, reminiscing on her College days, before she got married. She had joined an "Improv" group. She rehearsed with the group three nights a week, into the early hours of the morning. It was intense and exhausting, but the exhaustion was a healthy and exhilarating exhaustion. She ponders on other activities that she used to enjoy, and realises that she hasn't explored the creative side of her personality for quite some time.

She takes an introspective look at herself, writing rapid notes on her pad. She notices how large a part of her life is taken up with her work. There are many other aspects to life that she rarely considers. How does she prioritise her life – what comes first?

Her Work

Her Family

Her Self

9

Her Work

She decides to change some things. She is largely focused on results at work. Her time management leaves a lot to be desired. She is constantly under stress. Her workload is too heavy, but she never stands up for herself, or asks for help. She is working way too many hours. She is assuming responsibilities that she can not cope with. In fact, she is taking on other people's responsibilities as well as her own. Despite the fact that she is already well established in the firm, at times she feels more like a "Girl Friday". She begins to realise that her self-confidence is waning.

Her Family

Sandy realises that she is taking her family and family life for granted. Reflecting back on her marriage break-up with Ed, she recalls that many of the problems were due to the fact that she was rarely there, at important times in the family relationship; for example, Ed's promotion, her daughter's school picnic, parent-teacher meetings, going to the movies, etc. She had missed much of her daughters growing up, and was actually losing touch with who her daughter was becoming. Sandy feels bad, battling with the thoughts of being a bad mother and asks herself "how could things have got so out of control".

Her Self

As she began to ponder on herself, she notices that her clothes were the fashion of five years ago. Her glasses are broken and held together by scotch tape at the bridge. She touches her hair and noticed how unkempt it looks. After all she is always in a rush and generally just ties it back. Sandy wonders when was the last time that she had been on a 'decent' date with a member of the opposite sex. The memory seems somewhat vague. She notices a woman painting, and thinks carefully on the talents she loved and had stopped pursuing. She asks herself why, and answers herself by asking; "does it really matter". She is, however, jolted into the realisation that her life has to change sooner rather than later. She no longer wants to live in the world of "just doing."

Sandy makes the decision to re-prioritise.

Task:
How do you describe your work, your family and your self?
Below are a few ideas to help you get started...

1. Your Work
A place to grow and prosper
A place to make money
A way to define your place in the world ("I am a...")
Job satisfaction
A sense of achievement.
A means of building self confidence and self esteem
A way to serve the community
A place of enjoyment and fulfilment
Summer picnics, Christmas parties and other social occasions
A place to bully your subordinates
A place to be a subordinate and be bullied (some people love to
be a victim – they just don't know it)

2. Your Family
A place of nurturing
A place of development and growth
A place of belonging where your needs are met.
A place of safety and security
A place of comfort and laughter
A place of respite
A place of warmth and sanctuary
"A man's home is his Castle"
A woman's home is a place of love and connection
A battle field

3. Your Self
An opportunity to live
Freedom and liberty
Being on an exciting journey
The means to find happiness
An exploration of the universe
Boldly going where no one has gone before
Neggie Rapper (over thinking negatively)
A Dork.
A pain in the ass
A non conformist
A door mat
An empty vessel
A Soccer parent
A goddess or a freak
A desperate housewife
A nineties "Sex in the City" wannabe
A loner
An eternal optimist
Homer Simpson

Task:
How do you view your world?
Based on some of the ideas above how would you describe each
of the following;

Your Work
a) Positive aspects
....
....
....
b) Negative aspects
....
....
....

Your Family
a) Positive aspects

....
....
....

b) Negative aspects

....
....
....

Your Self
a) Positive aspects

....
....
....

b) Negative aspects

....
....
....

This is how Sandy has decided to reprioritise her world;

Her Self

Her Family

Her Work

Her Self
She goes to her family doctor for a check up. He does a full physical examination. He takes a number of tests, including, blood Cholesterol/HDL-Cholesterol (good Cholesterol)/LDL-Cholesterol (bad Cholesterol), Thyroid test, Liver and Kidney tests, blood sugar, and other tests he may feel appropriate. Following the results of these tests he may make suggestions for lifestyle change and/or medication. He suggests that she visit a nutritionist because she has a bad diet, and has a poor understanding of proper nutrition. He tells her that she needs to stop smoking, and recommends a number of aids to help her including hypnotherapy and acupuncture. He also suggests attending a counsellor on account of the high stress level in her life. When she says that she is "run down" he suggests reporting the driver to the police...

She goes to see a recommended nutritionist, who sits down with her and reviews her diet and lifestyle, over a cup of herbal tea and some muesli. She makes a food diary, following which her nutritionist is able to identify where she is doing well, and where her diet could be improved. She is given a recommended eating plan and lifestyle regime, which includes regular physical activity, of a type that she, is likely to enjoy, and hence stick with.

She is also given reading material and accompanying CD's, to educate her on nutrition. She is encouraged to concentrate less on her weight and more on healthy eating.

With the help of an experienced life coach she undergoes a series of self-exploration techniques. She begins by examining her belief system about herself and the world she lives in. In this way the coach is able to assist her in identifying negative beliefs about herself that have been hindering her from making positive life choices.

The coach then helps her identify her strengths and weaknesses and suggests that she maximise on her strengths and begin to work on her weaker aspects. The coach explains how she can learn to cultivate her so-called "weaknesses" into strengths.

Some of the weaknesses Sandy described were lack of motivation, leaving things until the last minute to get done, and shyness. Her coach educated her on skills that she was able to use immediately, to help her overcome some of these personal drawbacks.

During this process, she assists Sandy in putting together short-term and long-term goals, with a specific plan of action, which excites Sandy. She also helps her plan and manage her time better.

She attends a counsellor. She is careful to find one who comes recommended by many of his clients, and does not just pick one out of the "Yellow Pages".

Her counsellor helps Sandy to look at her life. She learns stress management skills and how to deal with any unfinished issues from her past. During her counselling sessions she discovers that she was constantly criticising her ex-husband (poor old Ed) and rarely expressing her own feelings. Now she realises that all he ever wanted to do was help her, but he just didn't know how and she never told him. Sandy is now realising that this is a behavioural pattern that she repeats in work and with her daughter too. She is learning assertive skills and self-care. Now, for the first time in Sandy's life, she feels in control.

Her Family
She takes one day out, each week, to spend quality time with her daughter Jamie. She asks her about her friends at school, her achievements, and any problems she has at school. They play music together (though she realises that Jamie will be too good for her very soon)

When Sandy was younger she was always fascinated by her father's camera. She decides to take up amateur photography and declares her daughter Jamie to be the perfect subject. From now on Sandy collects photographs of Jamie's cooking activities in the kitchen, going out on her first dance, shopping for clothes, washing the dog, strolling in the park, sleeping like a baby and being grumpy at breakfast time. Jamie loves the attention and positive interaction that Mom's photo hobby creates for them both. They decide to take up horse riding and ice-skating. They go out for dinner once a week where they discuss what's been going on in their week. Vowing never to miss a recital again Sandy feels proud of her daughter and looks forward to the time they spend together.

Her Work
She plans a meeting with her boss. In this meeting they discuss her work/home balance and how to reorganise/disperse her work load. They decide to organise a stress management course for all the staff in the organisation. She tells him that she needs certain days off to spend with her daughter. Options brought up include job sharing, flexitime and a wider choice of food in the Cafeteria (including Muesli).

Sandy still looks forward to Enrique's Tex Mex stand as a treat that she truly feels she deserves and guess what? Enrique asks her out on a date. She discovers that he is opening a franchise and helps him with some healthier options for his menu.

Sandy now feels back in charge of her own world, and is much happier, and contented. She enjoys a healthy work-life balance; looks forward to going to work and coming home, and gets to spend time with her daughter as she grows up.

Of course, not everything is fixable in the short term. Even achieving this much can take time. The most important thing is to identify the problems, set appropriate life-goals and plan realistic methods of attaining those goals

Task
In what order do you reprioritise your world (your work, your self, and your family)?

....

....

....

Under each heading, write down specifically how you intend to make changes, e.g. visit a doctor, nutritionist and/or life coach. Spend more time with your kids; change your diet; become more informed about lifestyle, activity etc....

1..
....
....
....
....

2..
....
....

....
....

3...
....
....
....
....
....

Often time's people feel that there is one thing in their lives that needs to be addressed. As you may have noted with Sandy, she needed to address various parts of her life, in order to get her desired outcome – to feel healthier and more in control of her life.

Earlier in this chapter we mentioned "work/life" balance. This seems to assume that work is not part of your life. Maybe a better expression would be "work-life integration"

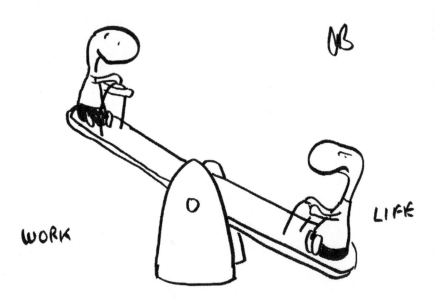

WORK   LIFE

Something to think about..
Write 5 lines on each of the following headings...

What are you doing that is not good for your health? E.g. nutritionally, lifestyle, work style
....
....
....
....
....

What are you doing that is good for your health? E.g. nutritionally, lifestyle, workstyle
....
....
....
....
....

What did you have for your lunch today? What??? You can't be serious. You ate that???..
....
....
....
....
....

What type of food do you eat when you are "on the run"
....
....
....
....
....

What is a "proper" meal to you, and how often do you have it?

....

....

....

....

....

Write down your ideal lunch

....

....

....

....

....

Write down your ideal stress free lunch

....

....

....

....

....

Make a decision on how you intend to incorporate a good nutritious lunch

....

....

....

....

....

(It doesn't matter if you don't get it right all the time, but at least now you are more aware of what you are eating and doing)

Are you stressed?
Sit down with a pen and paper in a quiet place and write down
everything that is bothering you.

....
....
....
....
....
....
....
....
....
....

Well done!
You have now converted a never-ending sea of problems to a
finite and limited list of problems on a page. It already seems
more manageable, doesn't it?

Now go through your list and remove all the things that you
can do nothing about (e.g. an asteroid is about to hit the earth
and we are all going to die! Your mother in law is about to visit,
the weather, the traffic, public transport, your favourite team
losing, your partner hogging the remote control, Pizza arriving
late)

Now go through what is left of your list and find all the things
that someone else can deal with, for you. They may make a
mess of them at first, but after a while they will do them without you. (E.g. all that photocopying, picking up your laundry,
going to the phone shop, getting the car valeted, housekeeping,
grocery shopping, picking up the brats, scanning documents,
answering the phone, getting the other half to go to the mall,
taking the garbage out)

Finally "never do today what you can leave until tomorrow".
Place all the things that you have to deal with - but don't have

to deal with today - on another list, and put it away until tomorrow. (E.g. washing the car, cutting the grass, all that filing, rearranging the furniture, requisitioning forms, emptying the dishwasher or clothes drier, returning phone calls). You will probably find that by tomorrow, someone will have already taken care of some of them.

Now you will be left with a small list of things that you alone have to deal with and that have to be dealt with today. It is better to have a small group of tasks that you can do well, than to be running around, chasing your tail, trying to do a hundred and one items at once.

Prioritise, delegate and make it so.

"The long span of the bridge of your life is supported by countless cables called habits, attitudes, and desires. What you do in life depends upon what you are and what you want. What you get from life depends upon how much you want it—how much you are willing to work and plan and cooperate and use your resources. The long span of the bridge of your life is supported by countless cables that you are spinning now, and that is why today is such an important day. Make the cables strong!"

L.G. Elliott

Section 2

PHYSICAL HEALTH
LET'S GET PHYSICAL

"When health is absent, wisdom cannot reveal itself, art cannot manifest, strength cannot fight, wealth becomes useless, and intelligence cannot be applied" -

Herophilus

When most people think about their health they think of their physical health. Physical, mental and emotional health states are all important. Problems with any aspect of your health will affect all other aspects of your health ("All for one and one for all!!!"). Unfortunately we tend to think of our health in a hierarchy of physical health first, then mental health and finally emotional health. This is a mistake, and often means that we concentrate on the first, and disregard the others.

All for one...!!!

We will discuss all three, as well as other important factors affecting our health, but at all times we will try to show how everything interacts and that no one aspect of our lives should be considered outside the context of the whole. We will try to always consider the whole - to be *Holistic*.

In this chapter we will discuss physical health, but hopefully as you read this and the following chapters you will realise that there are no sharp divides between the various aspects of our health.

Case History:
George is a butterball and an alcoholic. He used to play soft-ball, but now the only sport in his life is on the TV. He used to have a six-pack abdomen, but now the six-pack is on the floor beside the couch. His wife Gladys is 320lbs and 5' 2" tall. Their staple diet is chicken nuggets, pizza and fries. They are both in their early thirties, and are unlikely to see sixty. Their exercise regime consists of fighting over the TV remote. They both smoke up to 50 cigarettes a day. How can anybody be this unhealthy these days???

George works on a production line that involves him sitting all day long shifting empty boxes. He has a reputation amongst his fellow workers of being a slacker. No one likes to share his shift, as they have to work much harder to make up for him. He also smells bad, like rancid bacon, which does not endear him to his co-workers. George is not supposed to smoke on the production line, but he has found ways to surreptitiously have a drag every so often. His workmates are not impressed with this either as it is a fire risk, but so far he has got away with it.

Gladys rarely gets out of bed before midday. She finishes off what is left over from last nights chicken nuggets for breakfast. She washes down the congealed grease with a can of flat Cola. She looks at the dirty dishes, building up in the sink over the last few days.

She used to think about her appearance, and tried to look as well as she could. Now she doesn't really care. She used to enjoy spending hours getting ready, to go out. Now she never goes out, so there doesn't appear to be any point getting ready...

GEORGE AND GLADYS

Most people, like George and Gladys, do not intentionally try to damage their physical health. It is more like a few bad habits being left to become many bad habits. They get into a "rut"...

It does not take much effort to maintain your physical health, but some people take their health for granted. They just gradually take on more and more bad habits, none of which on their own are particularly harmful. Having one portion of fries and an (un) happy meal, does no harm on the odd occasion. Having them every night is another matter altogether. Add in a sedentary life style – "It's your turn to take the dog for a walk". "He looks so happy it is a shame to wake him..." – and you have the beginning of a health time bomb... Now wash that down with a few cocktails....

Of course, the first step in solving physical health problems is to realise that these problems exist in the first place. Sometimes people don't realise they have a problem. Sometimes they do, but they don't want to admit that they do.

"I have a lump in my breast. My mother had breast cancer. I don't want to have breast cancer. If I ignore the lump it will go away. So long as I don't find out that that is breast cancer, it isn't breast cancer..."

BURYING YOUR HEAD IN THE SAND
DOESN'T ALWAYS PREVENT YOUR BUTT GETTING
KICKED

"I have a toothache. I am terrified of dentists, because they are all sadists from "The Marathon Man". I also hate the sound of drills, because it sounds like they are drilling into my head... If I ignore this toothache it will go away, and I won't have to have any drills..."

"Love cures people - both the ones who give it and the ones who receive it."

Dr.Karl Menninger

Tasks

When considering your physical health, try using these headings:

Food Regime:
1. Keep a food diary
2. Check your food intake against the food pyramid.
3. Remember that you are not likely to stick to a diet that you don't enjoy. Find a healthy balance between what is good for you and what you enjoy.

Activity:
1. Try to do something active for at least 20 minutes, every day
2. Gradually increase the amount of physical activity you undertake.
3. Remember that you are not likely to stick to an activity that you don't enjoy.

Family history
Your family medical history can be relevant in a number of ways
1. Hereditary illness – You may inherit genes that may make certain conditions more likely e.g. diabetes, high cholesterol (with resultant risk of heart disease).

"Health is worth more than learning."

Thomas Jefferson

Alternative / complementary therapies.
Once diagnosis and medical intervention is established, it can be helpful to investigate suitable complementary therapies that can assist in recovery to, and maintenance of good physical help. They also help in the prevention of possible discomfort or increased symptoms in the future. The general objective is to improve energy levels, ease emotional and physical ailments and help create clarity of mind, feeling of well being, and self care. The focus is on self healing and utilising the innate power of intuition. Learning to take control of health by understanding

how the body/mind and spirit connection works, what enhances health and well being, how the mind can help heal the body and visa versa. Complementary therapy is especially effective in the reduction and management of stress, which is a major contributor to illness today.

As with all decisions in life it is important to choose a therapy that feels right to you and for you. Complimentary treatments should be used as part of, and in addition to, conventional "medical" methods.

Below is a list of complimentary therapies and benefits.

> *"Health is not valued till sickness comes."*
> Dr. Thomas Fuller

Acupuncture:
This is an ancient Chinese therapy which is used for almost all ailments. It is based on the theory that there are energy channels that run through the body. By means of very small needles, acupuncture helps unblock energy to help restore the body's natural state of chi (life force). It is excellent in the prevention of illness and the alleviation of symptoms e.g. anxiety respiratory, physical pain and emotional depression and high blood pressure. It is also used in the treatment of addictions like alcohol abuse, smoking, and weight problems. Also, it is highly regarded in the treatment of cancer and as a preparation for invasive surgery.

Ayurveda:
Ayurvedic medicine is an ancient Eastern system of health care. The word ayus means "long life" and veda means "knowledge" or "science". Based on the holistic belief that good health is measured by physical, mental, social and spiritual harmony, Ayurveda is beneficial in the prevention of illness as well as treatment for illnesses such as, cancer, asthma, arthritis, diabetes, ME etc,.

Aromatherapy:

This is an olfactory therapy that is used to stimulate the senses through smell and massage. It helps in relieving pain, skin infections, headaches, cold, asthma, colic, respiratory ailments, acne, and fatigue etc.

Herbalism:

Herbs can help to treat common complaints like acne, eczema, digestive disorders, irritable bowel syndrome, colitis, indigestion, psoriasis, high blood pressure, insomnia, stress, influenza and some allergic responses. Many modern medical treatments were developed from herbal preparations.

Homeopathy

Homeopathy is a form of preventative medicine, which attempts to correct functional disturbances before signs of disease have an opportunity to develop. This therapy is recognised world wide. Flower and plant derived toxins, known to produce the symptoms to be treated are prepared. These preparations are then diluted to the point where there is no toxin left in the solution. According to practitioners, the water retains the "water memory" of the toxin, and this is then used to treat the condition. This can play a significant role in the persons self care regimen both in prevention and healing.

Hypnosis:

Hypnosis can be practiced with the individual or with a group of people. Purposes vary and hypnosis can be applied to help control anxiety, physical and emotional pain, including distress and post traumatic disorder. Useful as an intervention for phobias and addictions, hypnotherapy can assist in almost all health related issues and lifestyle changes. It is recommended that self hypnosis is learnt and incorporated in a lifestyle regime as an excellent means of self care, relaxation and stress management.

Massage therapy:
This is a hands on therapy, which helps in relaxing, soothing, invigorating, and energising the muscles and connective tissue.

Nutritional Counsellor/Dietician:
This is an ideal approach to understanding good nutrition and how it affects health and well being. Many problems can happen due to the lack of knowledge as well as a lack of interest in personal health and vitality. The human body is an exquisite mechanism created to provide the highest level of health and healing.

A nutritional counsellor provides a sympathetic ear, and advice on lifestyle and dietary issues. This may involve sudden illness, requiring special diets and/or food allergies. It is important to note that many people who drastically change their diet can cause various physical difficulties and untold harm to themselves. Dietary changes should always be supervised by a medical professional. A change in diet is often, or usually necessary with problems such as arthritis, bowel and bladder disease, coronary artery disease, diabetes, high blood pressure, obesity, eating disorders, vegetarianism, food intolerance's etc

By assisting in nutritional and caloric education it becomes easier to follow through with healthy eating habits which can also include weight loss and maintenance. Small changes that are maintained are ultimately better than drastic changes that are short term.

Osteopathy:
This is a hands-on approach applied in the treatment of injury and pre-existing physical problems. Its aim is to enhance physical well being by strengthening the musculoskeletal framework, in addition to joints, muscles and spine.
It is suitable for all ages groups including infants.

> *"The sovereign invigorator of the body is exercise, and of all the exercises walking is the best".*
> Thomas Jefferson

Physiotherapy:
Physiotherapy also referred to as physical therapists involves the diagnosis and treatment a range of diseases, disorders, and disabilities. Physiotherapy is recognised in conventional medicine, so the medical profession can and regularly refer patients to them as part of a person's recovery treatment. Problems include related injuries after road traffic accidents, spinal, muscular and joint problems.

Personal Trainer:
With a bit of extra cash this is an absolute luxury to help getting active and fit. At the onset a profile is established by means of personal medical and lifestyle history, BMI (body mass index) and/or height/waist (weight) ratio is identified. Then an individual physical work out regime is designed including lifestyle and nutritional guidelines. A daily/weekly schedule is developed which can include cardio-vascular exercise and weight-training workouts. As an added benefit a Personal Trainer helps motivate, monitor and improve fitness levels. Remember you are your own best personal trainer: set realistic goals (nothing fancy); believe in your ability and follow through. A daily twenty minute walk is an excellent way to begin.

"A good laugh and a long sleep are the best cures in the doctor's book."

Irish proverb

Reflexology:
This is another hands-on therapy usually applied to the feet and hands. It provides many benefits for problems like arthritis, indigestion, general malaise, hormonal imbalance, pre menstrual syndrome, menopausal symptoms and a variety of other problems.

Tai - Chi

An ancient Chinese movement derived from martial arts. By means of the gentle and easy movements involved, tai-chi provides a gentle exercise to help achieve muscle tone and flexibility in the joint area. Tai-chi is suitable for pregnant women, overweight, and concvalesants. Tai – chi is an excellent and graceful exercise and is said to help create balance clarity and relaxation for all ages.

Medical conditions that are avoidable

Diabetes/Obesity

Type 1 diabetes mellitus

Type 1 (insulin dependant) diabetes is usually due to a genetic predisposition or to a viral infection affecting the pancreas, though insulin dependence in type 2 diabetes may result from poor compliance with treatment,

Type 2 diabetes mellitus

Type 2 (non insulin dependant) diabetes usually develops in middle age. A general observation says that about 90-95 % of people suffering with diabetes are type 2; about 80 percent are **Overweight:** Type 2 Diabetes Mellitus is more common among people who are older; obese; have a family history of diabetes and have had gestational diabetes. (2008 *www.diabetesinformationhub.com/WhatCausesDiabetes.php*)

A sedentary lifestyle, poor exercise, stress and poor diet are deciding factors related to developing diabetes and obesity.

> *"The human body has been designed to resist an infinite number of changes and attacks brought about by its environment. The secret of good health lies in successful adjustment to changing stresses on the body".*
>
> Harry J. Johnson

Body image/anorexia/bulimia/depression

Cardiovascular disease, high blood pressure, angina, Heart attacks, strokes, clots, high cholesterol, varicose veins, phlebitis, arterial disease.
Proper nutrition including plenty of vitamins and minerals are essential to a healthy cardiovascular system. The heart is like a thoroughbred horse and needs exercise. So make sure that you are getting plenty of aerobic exercise and relaxation. There is research suggesting that sodium intake should be minimised as there is salt added to most foods that we eat these days. High blood pressure is also a factor in heart disease.

Dental, gum disease, decay, and pre-mature teeth loss.

Dental caries/bad breath:
Recent research shows how poor dental hygiene can result in heart disease that is now a leading cause of death in both men and women. Gum disease is a bacterial infection causing gums to bleed easily and allows the bacteria to enter the bloodstream. Bacteria can attach itself to the fatty deposits in the heart blood vessels and can cause blood clots and may lead to heart attack. An associated condition called bacterial endocarditis is an infection of the heart valves and can be life threatening.

Since good oral health is integral to overall physical health, brush and floss properly and see your dentist or dental hygienist for check-ups on a regular basis. *Mark it as a reminder to do things in your diary or phone.* Word to the wise: *don't wait for the pain of a decay to occur before you visit your dentist.*

Gastritis, gastro-enteritis, flatulence, colitis, cancer
There may be certain foods that irritate your stomach, intestines and bowels. If so, then it's best to avoid them. A diet high in salt and processed foods is ill advised. A diet low in fruit and veggies should have those increased. Over drinking of alcohol, smoking and stress and anxiety plays a serious role in declin-

ing health of the entire body and well as contributing to gastric problems and cancer

> *"The only way to keep your health is to eat what you don't want, drink what you don't like, and do what you'd rather not. Thanks to Alan Bennett "*
>
> Mark Twain

Asthma, chronic bronchitis, emphysema

It is crucial that you don't blame yourself for an illness that you might get. Illness has a way of teaching us about ourselves and ensuring that we take greater care of ourselves. It's true that if you smoke cigarettes, ignore chest coughs and colds etc that you are likely to develop worse cases of the conditions as written above. Prevention is better than cure. If you smoke; find a quit smoking support group and develop a stress management course for yourself and stick to it.

Case History:

Bob is a med student. He is in his second year in medical school. He studies through the night and parties hard on week ends. Rugby bores him and he prefers to hang out in the library and cram. Since he has an exceptionally high IQ he really doesn't need to study so hard. However he has always been a high achiever, and does not know any other way to be.

He doesn't live on campus and his idea of cooking is opening a can of baked beans or scrambling eggs in the microwave. Bob drinks coffee, and eats on the run. He heard somewhere that as long as he eats carbs, he will have lots of energy.

He has a wiry scrawny appearance. He is under a lot of pressure, but much of the pressure is self imposed. His father is a well established surgeon with a large respectable private practice, and even though his father has never put him under any pressure, he feels he has a lot to live up to. He has always been a high achiever, but since he entered medical school, he finds his peers are more difficult to out-perform.

He is fit, but does not partake in sports, because he knows that he would not be the best, and if he can't be the best, he would rather not get involved. There is too much else to do. He also finds that physical activity is somewhat painful, and uncomfortable.

He regularly gets headaches, but puts that down to the pressure that he is under. He also has constant back pain, which is partially due to his long standing scoliosis. He gets a lot of heartburn, but he puts this down to his diet and constant ingestion of strong black coffee.

He is sociable, but generally prefers to stay apart from his fellow students, and is considered somewhat of a loner. Nobody actually dislikes him, but he does not seem to have any close friends either.

There are times that he lacks energy and motivation, but he puts that down to "the way he is", and tells himself to "just get on with it". Someday he will look into it, but for the moment he is just too busy...

Diagnosis:
Bob is stressed. He has a driven personality type. Even though much of Bob's stress is self imposed, he considers many of the non self-imposed stress as challenges to face up to. He will not admit to himself that he is stressed, so obviously he is not taking any measures to reduce that stress. In many ways Bob is addicted to stress, and would be very anxious in a world without stress. Bob's stressful lifestyle is how he identifies himself. *The more stressed he is, the more important he feels.*

Impending doom:
Bob has no sense of his own impending doom. Part of his problem is that he doesn't realise what is happening to him. Without identifying the problem, there is no prospect of identifying the

solution. Bob is physically well, but constant stress will ultimately affect his physical health. He may not suffer the consequences until he is middle aged, but, then again, he may have a mental or physical breakdown as soon as next week.

Stress is a health time-bomb. A certain amount of stress is necessary to motivate and stimulate us, and is very healthy. A life without stress would be very boring. When stress reaches a certain level, we find that we can cope, but it no longer produces an increase in productivity. After this point, increasing stress is no longer useful, and becomes increasingly unhealthy.

Worst case scenario.
As stated previously, Bob does not realise he has a problem, and consequently does not realise he needs a solution. He rationalises the multiple small problems that he experiences, and puts off any attempt at sorting them out. He is *an ostrich.* He has his head stuck firmly in the sand. What he has forgotten is that he can still get his ass kicked....

Best case scenario...
Bob either realises by himself, or somebody lets him know, that he has a problem. He examines his life and lifestyle. Most of his problems are actually minor, and can be resolved and/or prevented with a number of small lifestyle changes. He joins a number of student clubs (e.g. the chess club, a sports club or a drama group). He joins the college health centre, and with the help of a trainer starts a health and fitness regime. He starts to socialise more, and to make friends. His life becomes more balanced, and without even purposely doing anything about it, he finds his stress levels have reduced. He is much happier, and gets a lot more done.

> *"Laughter is the most healthful exertion."*
> Christoph Wilhelm Hufeland

Case History:

Lucy Cacopopolous is an anorexic and she doesn't realise it. Her body weight is 90lbs and her height is 5ft 4inches. Overconsumed by her physical appearance she is obsessed by her "fat" body image and is constantly finding new ways to conceal her thinness. She hides herself in oversized sweaters and shirts. Constantly comparing her body with those of her peers and local celebrities, she is never satisfied. Mentally devouring glossy pictures of rich, fattening foods in cookery books she longs to eat but knows she cannot and will not. Instead she distracts herself by being captain of the girls hockey team and an almost marathon walker around the soccer pitch in her free time. Lucy takes every opportunity to move her body ensuring to metabolise and work off every conceivable calorie that could possibly pass her lips. She rises at the crack of dawn to exercise ensuring never to lift weights, as she can't distinguish the difference between body fat and muscle. It fills a gap between her bones and skin and so it must be fat! Every movement is a deliberate exercise routine. It feels at times that she is dancing on the edge of an abyss. She eats sliced portions of fruit for her breakfast, fruit for her lunch and a meagre salad for dinner. Only ever drinking black coffee, her main evening meal is balanced with lean meats and salad, although she ensures that the portions are small. She calculates what goes in and what goes out and rarely exceeds a daily caloric intake of 500 calories. Lucy's menstrual cycle is almost absent.

She lives a double life; on the outside everyone sees her as school prefect and die-hard activist for victims of bullying and under achievers. Inside she tires of her relentless hunger - pangs and social departure.

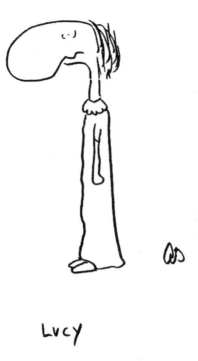

Lucy

Problems waiting to happen:
She could get seriously ill or even die, both in the short and long term
She could lose her normal menstrual cycle, and ultimately even become permanently infertile.
She could develop osteoporosis, and suffer from "brittle bones".
A low calcium intake will also cause dental problems, and abnormal musculo-skeletal development.

Anorexia is difficult to treat because:
- Oftentimes the person is unaware that they have a problem.
- Anorexics are not capable of helping themselves.
- There is no definite cut-off between "out of control" dieting and true anorexia, yet making that distinction is essential for early intervention.

Intervention
The first and most important step in intervention is a full medical and psychological assessment. It is important to document the diagnosis, and assess any and all other anorexia related complications.

Anorexia was once recognised as a female slimming disorder in the middle of the last century. However it is well documented now, that teenage men and middle aged men and women are also prone to this dis–ease. Anorexia is a deep-seated physical and emotional dis-ease and it is also life threatening.

Due to the complexities of this condition medical and psychological help and support is essential including rigorous behavioural modification, reintroduction of food intake and psychotherapy. There are many programmes available and although the sufferer is the centre of attention in these scenarios and rightly so, it is important to note that the entire family suffers as well and family intervention therapy and support groups are helpful.

Case History:
Arnie is a body builder. He lives in a one-bedroom apartment and works as a keep fit instructor at the local "Big Al's" Gym. There he gets an opportunity to work out and help others in achieving their goals of sculptured physical contours and chiselled abs.

ARNIE

Arnies personal goal is to be a world class professional body builder and Mr. Universe is a dream to be realised. In the meantime he enjoys doing regular television commercials which functions as a welcome supplement to his income. Working in the gym he claims to be somewhat of an expert on exercise and nutrition and gives advice freely, exhibiting his body as an example of health and physical perfection. Arnie is proud of his excellent physique and boasts that it is due to his controlled high protein diet and disciplined workout. He weighs 260lbs and explains that his daily caloric requirement is about 2500 calories per 100lbs body weight so his caloric intake is 6000 calories per day. That's why he takes protein supplements in the form of shakes, powders and bars. His diet contains proteins, carbohydrates and fats.

Proteins are: cheese, meats, fish, milk, soya, eggs and nuts etc.
Carbohydrates include potatoes, rice, bread, fresh fruits and vegetables.
Fats include oily fish, olive and flaxseed oil, avocado, cheese and nuts.

He eats five to six small meals a day. He never eats processed foods or junk foods and always avoids high sugar fruit juices and sodas. He drinks plenty of water though.

So what do you think of these fad diets? Arnies high protein and Bob's high carb and Lucy lu's leavery?

Any advice for Arnie?

How (what) is your physical shape
Apples and Pears

....

....

....

....

Are you proud or embarrassed to undress in the department store communal changing rooms, on the beach, or at the local swimming pool?

....
....
....
....

Reasons Why:
....
....
....

When is the last time you got serious about managing your eating habits better?
....
....
....
....

On a scale from 1 – 10, 10 being extremely fit, where do you rate yourself?
....
....
....

Healthy Eating
Non- vegetarian

FOOD PYRAMID

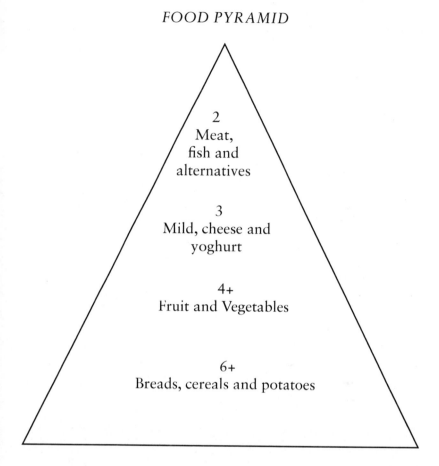

2
Meat,
fish and
alternatives

3
Mild, cheese and
yoghurt

4+
Fruit and Vegetables

6+
Breads, cereals and potatoes

Plan your daily meals with foods from each section of the food pyramid, starting from the bottom

Eat mostly:
Fruit, vegetables, salads, peas, beans, lentils, cereals and potatoes

Eat moderately:
Low-fat yogurt, low-fat milk, low-fat cheese, nuts, fish, lean meat, chicken without skin, eggs

Eat small amounts:
Butter, oil, spreads, sugar and salt

Eat only very occasionally:
Confectionary, chips, chocolate, cakes, cookies and pastry

Take freely
Cereal Food:
Whole-wheat, oatmeal, bread, wholegrain rice and pasta, cereals

Drinks:
Decaffeinated tea and coffee, herbal teas, mineral water, fruit juices, clear soups, home made veg and lentil soups

Eggs and Dairy Foods:
Skimmed milk, low-fat milk, e.g. cottage and curd cheese. Egg whites

Fats:
All fats should be limited

Fish:
All white fish, and oily fish

Fruits and Vegetables:
All fresh and frozen vegetables. Dried beans and lentils are very high in fibre. Jacket potatoes – eat skins. Fresh and dried fruit and vegetables.

Made up Dishes:
Skimmed or low-fat: milk puddings, sauces, custard. Jelly, sorbet and meringue.

Meat:
Lean meat, chicken, turkey, veal, and poultry

Preserves and Sweets
Bovril, marmite, Vegemite, boiled candy, fruit pastilles, peppermints etc, jam, marmalade, honey, molasses and sugar.

Note:
ADVISABLE *foods are generally low in fat or high in fibre or both. These should be used regularly as part of your eating plan.*

In Moderation
Cereal Food:
White flour, white bread, white rice pasta.

Drinks:
Packet soups, Alcohol

Eggs and Dairy Foods:
Edam cheese, low fat cheddar, low fat cheese slices/spread, 3 egg yolks per week.

Fats:
Margarine labelled high in polyunsaturated fats, corn oil, sunflower oil, safflower oil, and olive oil.

Fish:
Shell fish occasionally (unless you are allergic)

Fruit and vegetables:
Avocado pears and olives

Meat (Lean):
Meat, fish pastes, ham, beef, pork, lamb, bacon, lean mince

Nuts:
Almonds, Brazil nuts, chestnuts, hazelnuts, peanuts, walnuts and peanut butter.

Made up Dishes:
Ice-cream, pastry puddings, scones, cakes and cookies made with suitable margarine or oil.

NOTE:
Foods in MODERATION contain *polyunsaturated fats or smaller quantities of saturated fats. As your eating plan should be low in fat, these foods are allowed only in moderation.*
For example,
a) red meat three times/week;
b) medium fat cheeses and meat and fish pastes once a week; and
c) home made cakes, biscuits and pastries made with appropriate polyunsaturated margarine or oil, twice a week.

Saturated fats are triglycerides (fats) where there are only single bonds between the carbon atoms in the chain.

$$H - \underset{\underset{H}{|}}{\overset{\overset{H}{|}}{C}} - \underset{\underset{H}{|}}{\overset{\overset{H}{|}}{C}} - \underset{\underset{H}{|}}{\overset{\overset{H}{|}}{C}} - \underset{\underset{H}{|}}{\overset{\overset{H}{|}}{C}} - H$$

Unsaturated fats are triglycerides (fats) where there are one (monounsaturated) or more (polyunsaturated) double bonds between the carbon atoms in the chain.

$$H - C = C = C - C - H$$

with H atoms branching from the carbons:

$$
\begin{array}{cc}
H & H \\
/ & / \\
H - C = C = C - C - H \\
/ & / \\
H & H
\end{array}
$$

Unsaturated fats have carbon bonds available for attachment of hydrogen atoms (hydrogenation). The more hydrogenation the more saturated the triglyceride or fat becomes. Saturated and hydrogenated fats are more unhealthy.

Eat Rarely
Cereal Foods:
Fancy breads e.g. croissants, savoury cheese biscuits, and cream crackers

Drinks;
Cream soups

Eggs and Dairy Foods:
Whole milk, cream, hard cheese, cream cheese

Fats:
Butter, margarine high in saturated fat, cooking/vegetable oil of unknown origin.

Fish:
Fish roe, fried fish

Fruit and Vegetables:
Potato chips

Made up Dishes:
Whole milk puddings, dairy ice-cream, pastry puddings, cakes, cookies, biscuits and sauces made with whole milk, eggs or

inappropriate fat or oil. All proprietary puddings and sauces. Mayonnaise.

Meat:
Visible fat on meat (including crackling), sausages, paté, duck, goose, streaky bacon, meat pies, meat pastes.

Nuts:
Coconut

Sweets, Preservers and Spreads:
Chocolate, toffees, fudge, butterscotch, lemon curd, mincemeat.

Note:
Foods NOT ADVISED contain large proportions of saturated fats and therefore should be avoided wherever possible.

NOTE: IF YOU ARE OVERWEIGHT, FOODS HIGH IN SUGAR SHOULD BE AVOIDED AND USE OF APPROPRIATE FATS AND OILS SHOUILD BE LIMITED.

SAMPLE MENU
CHOLESTEROL LOWERING DIET

BREAKFAST
Fresh Fruit/Fruit juice unsweetened, porridge/wholegrain cereal wholemeal, Bread tea/coffee.

DINNER
Clear soup or fruit juice, fish, poultry or lean meat, vegetables/salads potatoes – boiled or baked. Fresh fruit/low fat desert tea/coffee.

LUNCH/DINNER
Fish lean meat/low fat cheese/pulse vegetables/(beans/lentils) dish. Salad/vegetables. Whole-wheat bread. Fresh fruit. Tea/coffee.

SNACKS
Tea/coffee/fruit juice/fresh fruit plain cookies if desired. Water

"And if I do this will I live forever?..."
"No... But it will seem like it!"

Average Portions
Fish and poultry: 4 ounces (113g) cooked weight
Lean meat: 3 ounces (85g) cooked weight

COOKING
Steaming, baking, braising and grilling of food is recommended. Frying should be kept to a minimum with small amounts of un-saturated oil, e.g. corn or sunflower oil. Many foods may also be cooked without fat in a microwave oven or on a non-stick pan

IT IS RECCOMMENDED THAT YOU DRINK TWO LITRES (FOUR PINTS) OF WATER PER DAY

A "glass half full" approach would be to think in terms of "adding in" rather than "cutting out". If you eat more of the recommended food items, you will naturally eat less of the "not advised" food items, but you are less likely to crave them.

"Make your own recovery the first priority in your life."
Robin Norwood

Write 5 lines on each of the following headings...

What am I doing that is not good for my health?.
nutrition, lifestyle, workstyle (e.g. nutrition: balanced food intake; lifestyle: exercise and social life; work style: hours at work etc)

Nutrition:
....
....
....
....
....

Lifestyle:
....
....
....
....
....

Work style:
....
....
....
....
....

What are you doing that is good for your health? e.g. nutritionally: balanced food intake, lifestyle: exercise and social life, work style: hours at work etc

Nutrition:

....
....
....
....
....

Lifestyle:

....
....
....
....
....

Work style:

....
....
....
....
....

What did you have for your lunch today? **What??? You can't be serious. You ate that???..**

....
....
....
....
....

What type of food do you eat when you are "on the run"

....

....

....

....

....

What is a "proper" meal to you, and how often do you have it?

....

....

....

....

....

> *"Getting my lifelong weight struggle under control has come from a process of treating myself as well as I treat others in every way."*
>
> Oprah Winfrey

Tasks
Start a "food diary"
Without trying to change your diet, write down everything you eat and drink each day and make an notation of the time that you eat and drink it. Be very honest with yourself. This will be your "launch pad". This is where you are starting from...

Write down your ideal lunch

....

....

....

....

....

Write down your ideal stress free lunch

....
....
....
....
....

Make a decision on how you intend to include a good nutritious lunch in a stress free environment.

....
....
....
....
....

It doesn't matter if you don't get it right all the time. Start off with small steps, sometimes you get it and sometimes you don't. Pat yourself on the back for the times that you do get it right, and give yourself a motivating mental push for the times you get it wrong. E.g. tell yourself "I am on track" and build on your victories

"A man too busy to take care of his health is like a mechanic too busy to take care of his tools."

Spanish proverb

EMOTIONAL HEALTH
STOP WHINING –
WHO CARES ANYWAY...

"The starting point for a better world is the belief that it is possible. Civilisation begins in the imagination. The wild dream is the first step to reality. Visions and ideas are potent only when they are shared. Until then, they are merely a form of daydreaming."

Dr. Norman Cousins

Who or what would we be without our emotions? Perhaps we would be robots, or alien/Vulcan-like creatures, all sounding the same and performing tasks in the equivalent manner. Imagine a person without laughter and tears, a voice without inclination, a speech without passion or a rock concert without clamour, a world without feeling, devoid of emotion. It appears to us to be dull and boring, almost lifeless and colourless, stale and withered.

Part of what makes us uniquely human is the fact that we *can* feel, and not just in a tactile manner, as in holding someone's hand or petting a dog, but also by sympathising or empathising with a person's sadness or partaking in another's joy. We have varying degrees of emotion; some of which are anger, resentment, fear and hate. Others include exhilaration, ecstasy, enthusiasm, passion, and love. Love-relationships begin with emotion and end with emotion. In the beginning there is usually a high and volatile emotion and in the end there is a sense of disillusionment and grief. When a relationship continues it settles into an everyday routine. An example would be people who mate for life.

EMOTIONS

Everything we do in our life is driven by our emotions. In order for us to excel in what we do, we must feel motivated, determined, excited or fearful. We must get positive or negative feedback.

For example, often when people decide to take up a new musical instrument, they decide to buy a cheap instrument "in case they don't take to it". This is not a good idea. The world's best musician will sound terrible on a cheap instrument. How you sound is the biggest feedback you get from an instrument. If you sound bad, you will be discouraged, and will give up. But how do you know that it is not you, but the instrument that sounds bad? So always get the best instrument you can afford. You will always get a better resale value from a good instrument anyway...

In most of our life events, the feedback that drives us is emotional. We feel good/bad/indifferent, but we always feel something. Everything we do in life is based on our emotions - how we view the world; how safe we feel in the world, how comfortable we feel with people; how comfortable we are with investments; whether we trust people or not; how we feel about our government etc. We learn as we grow up to dismiss our emotions and focus more on the practical – logical rather than emotional feedback. This is not necessarily a bad thing. In an ideal world, emotional feedback tempers the logical and vice versa. If one ignores either feedback, the balance is lost

A term commonly used in NLP (neuro-linguistic-programming) is"*sensory acuity system*": We internally *re-present* what we see, hear, touch, smell and taste by means of our own individual history and belief system. For example when you see old photographs they stir up memories of happy or sad times gone by. When a mother gazes at pictures of her adult children, taken when they were toddlers, she feels a deep emotion of nostalgia, loss or love. Whenever I see Christmas cards of snowy landscapes it reminds me of the first time l played in the snow as a child. Making a snowman, so when I glance at Yuletide images I can't help but feel nostalgic.

When listening to unforgettable music or cherished poetry one automatically return's to the impassioned experiences on first hearing the music or reading the poem. The smell of home made bread or apple tart can awaken the emotions of a lost youth, when coming home from school or enjoying Sunday tea. The aroma of freshly cut grass on a summers evening, and the smell of piped tobacco in a room often invokes forgotten childhood memories. The vista of the Golden Gate Bridge has inspired generations. The effervescent taste of sparkling wine or champagne revitalises memories of celebrations and good times past. The touch or embrace from a loved one can remind you of precious warmth and comfort. Take a moment and reminisce upon special times in your life; For instance, a birthday party, a first kiss, a graduation, a favourite pet, a first home, a first shave, a first pay-check, a day at the sea side, a frosty beer, an ultra smooth martini or a magnificent fire work display. Think of some of your own special memories and notice the emotions that they conjure up for you.

- Make a list of great moments and memories from your far away or recent past.
- Along side them write down the corresponding emotions you felt:
- Then practice spending at least thirty seconds to a minute each visualising your most favourite ones.

....
....
....
....
....
....
....
....

Then of course we have our sixth sense, normally regarded as *intuition,* that wise and wizardly part of us that guides you and fine-tunes decision-making processes. Your intuition senses what is right for you and what you feel is right for others.

THE 6TH SENSE

Our lives are so busy these days. For many of us we oscillate between feeling motivated, hungry, stressed, agitated, depressed, worried and fatigued, with some stolen moments of fun in between. It is important to revitalise or revisit powerful and enjoyable feelings from your past. Every so often you must anchor yourself by calling upon these happy, relaxing or exciting emotions that your memory holds so clearly. Use the power of your own mind to re-connect and see, hear and feel your emotions again and again. We suggest that you make a habit of this because it is enjoyable and good for your health.

"Emotions are wild horses. It is not explanations that carry us forward, but our will to go on".

- Paulo Coelho Source: Life

Compassion

COMPASSION

Compassion is a word that is rarely used, yet it is vital to your health and well being. You can just about *survive* without compassion but you definitely cannot live a fulfilled life without it. People need to be able to feel compassion from you just as you need to feel it from them. So what is compassion anyway? Is it a thing that you do, something that you say or just a natural and innate feeling that comes from within? People show compassion in many ways. For example we show compassion by being thoughtful about other peoples' feelings; using tact in conversations; showing respect and being courteous towards others. Compassion is a way in which people communicate through their use of words, gestures and actions. For instance, someone tells you about a sad experience they had; a loss of any kind; you see a puppy with a wounded paw; a baby who cries from pain or hunger; people suffering in third world countries or your loved ones becoming ill or frail... How does it make you feel? Glad that it isn't you?

You may well succumb into a moment of empathy, connection and compassion towards these people, animals or circumstances. Your response could easily be that you want to fix the situation and make it better for them. You may want to listen attentively to their story; to witness the experience of what happened to them; to hold them close so that they feel safe and cared for, or simply be there with them without saying a word. Remember the saying "A problem shared is a problem halved". No matter how strong and virile you may become; no matter how self-assured and self-reliant you may be; regardless of how high you build your fortress around you, you cannot live without compassion in your life. In today's world you must remember how important you are to others and how necessary it is for you to be aware of other people's feelings.

It is not always easy to tell what someone is coping with in their life. Try not to assume that you know. Stay tuned into their frequency. You can give them a smile, make a joke and lighten their day. Ask them how they are and "listen" to their reply. In fact making someone laugh is worth more than gold. Don't judge – just listen. Expressing positive regard towards others is compassion. Practice it and never turn away or reject it from others. Welcome it into your life - you deserve compassion. It is warm and nice to receive some compassion when you're sad, hurt or lonely. How nice it is to know that someone cares about you, and how you feel.

"Empathy is the most radical of human emotions."
Gloria Steinem
(1934) Source: *Jamestown, N.Y., Post Journal*

Happiness

HAPPINESS

We have an incredible mechanism that has yet to be fully and scientifically understood. For example people are cured from life threatening illnesses when allopathic interventions are exhausted.

After many years of severe pain, suffering from a life threatening disease, international author and humanitarian Norman Cousins cured himself by following a regimen of high doses of vitamin C, positive emotions which included watching Marx Brothers movies, done in the full knowledge and support of his doctors.

In his book "Anatomy of Illness" Dr. Normal Cousins described how movies cured his disease. "Is it possible" he wondered "that love, hope laughter, confidence and the will to live have therapeutic value".

Cousins made sure that he enjoyed a hearty belly laugh for a few minutes each day. This, he said gave him more than sixty minutes of pain free sleep. Many credit the scientific study of the effect of humour on physical wellbeing to Dr. Norman Cousins and Dr. Patch Adams. Patch Adams is a medical practitioner, theatrical clown and activist. He devoted thirty years or more to creating changes to the healthcare system in the United States of America. He believed the healthcare system to be expensive and only available to the wealthy

For years, the use of humour has been used in medicine. Surgeons used humour to distract patients from pain. Medical doctors have found that children similarly can be effectively distracted with funnies, stories and the like.

Over the years, researchers have conducted studies to explore the impact of laughter on health. Studies have shown that moments of laughter helped to reduce pain, decrease stress-related hormones and boost the immune system.

The scientific literature acknowledges that laughter is a useful therapeutic intervention and can help improve the health of patients who are suffering from chronic illnesses including depression. Many hospitals in the United States, Canada, India and England now offer laughter therapy programs as complementary treatment.

So how does it work?
Laughter decreases blood pressure and alleviates anxiety, while triggering endorphins—the feel good chemicals of the body. It has been well established that laughter increases the sense of well being, while relieving stress, and generally contributes to better health.

Laughter, along with an active sense of humour, may help protect you against a heart attack, according to a study by cardiologists at the University of Maryland Medical Centre in

Baltimore. The study, which is the first to indicate that laughter may help prevent heart disease, was presented at the American Heart Association's 73rd Scientific Sessions on November 15 in New Orleans.

"The old saying that 'laughter is the best medicine,' definitely appears to be true when it comes to protecting your heart," says Michael Miller, M.D., director of the Centre for Preventive Cardiology at the University of Maryland Medical Centre. "We don't know yet why laughing protects the heart, but we know that mental stress is associated with heart attack.

Love

Clearly love is the fundamental birth right of all human beings. We cannot live wholly without a loving touch, smile, embrace or shared words. Love makes the world go around. All life, human, animal, and even plant, benefits from love. When you make dinner with care and contentment it tastes better!! *If you don't believe us try it...*

As we continue to explain how your emotions affect your general health and well being, it is equally important that you begin to recognise some of your own emotions that are not generously expressed or emotions that you suppress. Notably love is different for everyone especially at different stages of your life. The emotion of love is experienced in many ways, for example we can fall in love romantically, love a piece of music, love our siblings, parents, possessions, pets, control, our country, me time, a warm bath, a good party, movie and the list goes on. Let's examine what love is to you.

What do you love?
(e.g. career, travel, boat, toy soldiers, fishing, Internet surfing, candle lit dinners, privacy and solitude, etc)

....
....
....
....
....

How does each item on your list make you feel?
(e.g. determined, stimulated, relaxed, childlike, serene, adventurous, romantic, safe and secure, etc)

....
....
....
....
....

Who do you love?
(e.g. brother, sister, mother, father, partner, mistress, dog, yourself)

....
....
....
....
....

How does it make you feel to love each of the above?
(e.g. bonded, connected, nurtured, safe, secure/pressurised, excited, needed and unconditionally loved, at peace)

....
....
....
....
....

Love is a strong emotion and oftentimes people protect themselves from feeling its power and by becoming empowered by it. Holding back and staying protected is a familiar place that people can find themselves in. There are many reasons for this; sometimes it can be due to past traumas, rejection, messy divorces, low self - esteem or the first break up which remains a lasting blueprint for relationships to come. You can see and experience the pain of a loved one and swear vehemently that it will never happen to you or that you will never cause or contribute to the pain of another. There are times when you are scared that you may not feel the closeness or love from one or others again so you chase it like a crazy person and eventually sabotage its potential. Sometimes people sense true love and run away like scared bunny rabbits scurrying frantically into their little burrows. So we ask you, what is the difference between love and fear as each emotion is equally potent with specific influences on the body and mind. Each emotion plays a definite role in the health, healing and ageing process of individuals.

Ask yourself;
Are you being your authentic self in your relationships? Do you express how you feel in your Intimate, personal, work and social life?

Intimate: Yes [   ]No [   ]   Sometimes [   ]

Personal   Yes [   ]No [   ]   Sometimes [   ]

Work   Yes [   ]No [   ]   Sometimes [   ]

Social   Yes [   ]No [   ]   Sometimes [   ]

What have you discovered about yourself based on what you said above?
....
....
....
....
....

Love is often associated with sex and visa versa. In fact, depending on who you are having sex with, it can be anything. Sex in itself can be exciting and wonderful or degrading and discouraging. Much depends on your intentions for having sex in the first place. Apart from being in monogamous and loving relationships, nowadays people have sex for different reasons. Sometimes it is because they are lonely and sometimes it is because it makes them feel virile, desired and/or dominant. Sometimes people do it to procreate; Sometimes just to have fun. Be honest with yourself about your sexual practice or lack of same. For example, is sex meaningful or "pass-the-time-able"? Are you responsible in your sexual relationships? This implies being respectful of yourself and of the other person, and being reliable and trustworthy regarding contraception and STD's. Are you always honest about your intentions or will you say anything to get a guy or a gal into the sack? Are you the "Floosie in the Jacuzzi" or the "Top Cat" meowing around town or the "Hound – Dawg" howling from street corners?

Even though you don't have to be in love with the person(s) you sleep with, there is no feeling that can come close to waking up beside the person you love. By the way, meaningful sex is good for your, emotional, mental and physical health.

"Whatever you do ~ you will attract more of it"

How can you attract and receive more love into your life?
For example: are you grouchy, nasty and yell a lot at waiters, or do you make daisy chains and participate in global-warming-and-world-peace demo's?

....
....
....
....
....

Remember the caption that reads "Love is never having to say you're sorry". We disagree because no one gets it right all the time, so you ought to show some humility and respect to the other and apologise! Valentines and Hallmark days are inflated with endearing wishes to create loving emotions in others, or so it would appear. Although the sentiment is endearing the obligation defeats the purpose.

In any case we have chosen a few "Love – isms" to get you thinking about what this emotion means to you. Have a little fun with it, as we have.

Love is being honest with yourself and with others.
Love is knowing when to shut up, Love is acknowledging others for no particular reason, Love is respecting all of life
Love is keeping in touch with people who have zero influence on your career advancement or your status quo.
Love is taking care of yourself.
Love is not dropping your friends' Theremin.
Love is reading a good book.
Love is being considerate of others people's feelings.
Love is not having to ask "why".
Love is listening to an uninterrupted Chopin's piano concerto No. 1 in E minor
Love is walking and splashing about in the rain.
Love is sitting by the fire with family or friends on a cold wintry night.
Love is telling ghost stories and laughing out loud.
Love is giving someone your last of anything.
Love is lending someone your car.
Love is lending someone money and never expecting it back.
Love is forgiving someone and really meaning it.
Love is visiting the sick in hospital and courageously risking MRSA.
Love is paying your bills on time.
Love is having a party and inviting people who would like to be included.
Love is hearing someone sing off key and not saying a word or laughing hysterically.
Love is never telling your partner that they snore.
Love is allowing people to be themselves.
Love is never criticising yourself or others.
Love is never telling your friend or partner that they are fat, unfit or imperfect in anyway.

Love is thinking of how others might feel before you open your big trap and saying something completely stupid (or sometimes even keeping it shut).
Love is turning the night-light off so your partner can sleep.
Love is always saying please and thank you.
Love is being a silly Sally not a sour Sally! Love is being a merry Muffin not a Ratty Roland!
Love is anything you want it to be as long as you love yourself first.

Declare your own Love - isms below as you make some "Love is" quotes for yourself and write them here:

....

....

....

....

....

Forgivness

FORGIVENESS

You must forgive your mother. You must forgive your father. You must forgive your brother. You must forgive your sister. You must forgive yourself. You must forgive otherwise you will hurt yourself slowly but surely. Not forgiving yourself is self destructive. Oftentimes people think that by forgiving someone that they are letting them off the hook. You probably feel that the other person hasn't suffered enough and by not forgiving them it will be a form of retribution. Oh dear! You can't quite let by-gones be by-gone yet, so that you can move on with your life. So whom are you holding captive in your jailhouse? Do you think that now might be a good time to let them out? Are you ready to let them out? Who exactly is holding the torch for the pain? Chances are that the person is you and the other person has moved on and is dancing down the street living happily ever after!

We'll come back to that.... First let's examine the benefits of forgiveness for you in your life:

Peace of heart and peace of mind is freedom. Forgiveness is an experience that is unique for everyone. It is described as an innate 'releasing' experience. When we hold on to resentment towards another, or ourselves, our minds and bodies carry a heaviness or dead weight. It becomes physically obvious by our facial expressions, posture and conversation, or lack of same. When you forgive you set yourself free and the other too. Resentment and bitterness is an energy that once locked into can lead to fatigue depression and eventual illness. We have often heard of the amazing transformations people make in their lives when challenged with terminal illness. As part of their allopathic treatment, they usually follow a rigorous journey of emotional, as well as, or even instead of physical recovery. This includes invoking calmness and tranquillity into their lives by reconciliation with the past and creating peace with themselves as well as others. This involves taking time out and to become introspective by asking yourself self-effacing questions. This can best be achieved with the help and guidance of an experienced therapist and/or support group. However this does not guarantee that you will find complete inner peace but as part of your healing regimen it will surely move you forward and enhance your health and well being, no end. Of course, this does not mean that all ill-health is the end result of resentment and lack of forgiveness.

Take for example Louise Hay; a world class pioneer in self-development. She discovered that she had ovarian cancer. As well as undergoing conventional medical care, she put all of her teachings to the test and followed an in-dept regimen of self-care; forgiveness, love and acceptance. This worked because it is truly the way that she healed herself. Today, her experience and knowledge enriches people's lives all over the world, as described in her book, "You Can Heal Your Life"

There are many other great teachers of our time including one of our mentors Dr. Caroline Myss, who is emphatic in her writing and teaching, that forgiveness is important for the health of mind, body and spirit. In her book "Why people don't heal and how they can", she writes that *every illness is an opportunity to learn something more about myself* (p.166).

Caroline also discusses the important stages you must take in order to heal. You must learn to say "no" to others and "yes" to your needs. Healing is a present tense word and that action should start now, because 'tomorrow never comes'. You need energy today to help heal your illness today. When all your energy is focused on *"why did they do that?"*, *"It wasn't fair"*, *"I'll get my revenge"*, etc; Your vital energetic life force simply dribbles away and is no longer of any use to you whatsoever today!

"Your only task is to learn to forgive - and call back the energy you are wasting on events in the past"

Just for a moment ask yourself *"who in your life do you need to forgive?"* or *"who needs your forgiveness?"* initials will do!

....
....
....
....
....

Simply put, the longer you put off the act of forgiveness the longer you suffer internally either consciously or subconsciously. Perhaps you have a history of unresolved issues, that may not be resolved, It is essential to heal the wound as best you can, You are holding onto so much of the past, because that is where all your vital energy is going.

Give up the drive to know why but maintain an enjoyable curiosity.
Stop trying to uncover the mystery of your life, but remain fascinated by it.

Try to enjoy and accept things as they are. It has been said that a word of inspiration can take up to five years to take effect. This is because of the energy consumed by holding onto negative influences in your past.

Work through it and move on! It's on your mind not theirs after all and "frankly my dear they don't give a damn".

Let's get to the heart of the matter.

"LET'S GET TO THE HEART OF THE MATTER"

Ask yourself:
What did they do to you? *Be specific*
e.g. beat you with a stick, take your wife, steal your car, got the promotion instead of you, knock down your dog..

....

....

....

....

....

What actual event (or events) took place?
e.g. she/he had a sex change without telling you, she/he went off with someone else, (s)he ruined your business. (S)he killed your dog

....
....
....
....
....

What are they responsible for besides hurting your sensitive feelings?
e.g. disgracing you among your peers, making you bankrupt, causing you to end up in jail, destroying your reputation, leaving you dog-less.

....
....
....
....
....

Identify the emotional scars that you feel you are left with
e.g. I feel betrayed, abandoned, lost, humiliated, used, cheated, angry, sad/depressed, lonely, emasculated and lonely for the dog

....
....
....
....
....

Have you sustained these hurts by pondering, thinking and reminding yourself of the event or events over and over again? Repeating the same old questions as if they were some kind of mantra "why did this happen to me"? or "How could they have done such a thing"?

YES   [ ]
NO   [ ]

Identify what actually happened, not what happened to you?
There is a difference!

....
....
....
....
....

Its time to get real as everyone else will have long since forgotten the instance.

In Charles Dicken's "A Christmas Carol", Scrooge is taken on an emotional journey by three ghosts; the ghost of "Christmas past", the ghost of "Christmas present" and finally the ghost of "Christmas future". The ghost of "Christmas past" shows him the reality of his childhood and how he came to be the man he is. The ghost of "Christmas present" shows him the choices he has at the moment. The ghost of "Christmas future" shows him the possible outcomes of the choices he could make.

Let us take you on a journey, with your own three ghosts, along a road with many forks (or if you are Chinese then it will be a road with many chopsticks)

Think of something wonderful that has happened in your past. Now visualise it – make the picture bigger and see yourself there.

Now... think of a sad experience from your past. Again visualise it and make the picture bigger...

Focus on how happy and joyful you were in the first picture. Then focus on how miserable you were in the second picture.

Happiness and misery are both powerful experiences that develop your personality.

Look around you. See what is wonderful right now.

Now imagine an experience that can bring good feelings of excitement, joy and happiness into your life.

With these past present and future pictures, let the feelings run through your mind and body. Run that picture through your mind over and over again. Go with that good feeling..

Our experiences in the past are the basis on which we make decisions in the present, which will ultimately dictate the events in our future. We can use our experience of happiness in the past to guide us to happiness in the future, but in any event, we are the ones who make the decisions right now.

Daily Affirmations: "I retrieve and enjoy only good memories from my past" – "I focus on all positive events in my life"

Releasing the painful past:
First step: Acceptance. Whatever happened actually happened and it is just horrible, we get it! Regardless of how many times you ask, "why could this have happened to me?" It will not change anything in your life except the repeated subconscious satisfaction of torturing yourself endlessly as you analyse these events over and over again. Obviously, what has happened has happened, but emotionally it is still taking place in your mind, and you are feeling it in your body. It's true you're hurt, rejected and/or betrayed! You could feel like you've been run over by a freight train. It's over. The good thing about the past is that it is over. Cappiche, Finito, Deireanach! Dead and ended.

You are not your past, it's only an experience; an experience from which you can learn. The truth is that you are holding onto to it. As stated in the last few paragraphs, perhaps you are not thinking about these incidents or experiences "twenty-four seven", but you can easily recall and almost bring it back life in an instant.

Accept that and begin by affirming
"I am now willing to forgive ....
....
....
....
....
...."

You are not your past. You are free to change once you forgive and accept your right to change.

Affirm: *"I am not my past; I am a person capable of changing and turning away from past patterns of behaviour".*

> *"Realise that now, in this moment of time, you are creating. You are creating your next moment based on what you are feeling and thinking. That is what's real."*
>
> Doc Childre

"Why people don't heal and how they can",
Caroline Myss,
1998, p.166, p.172, Batham Press

ARCHETYPES
WHO SHALL I BE TODAY?

An archetype is a universal pattern encoded in what Carl Jung referred to as our collective unconscious. Jung believed that we all share ancient behavioural patterns that are held in the subconscious and become apparent because they are repetitive. Similar to beliefs, you can recognise these archetypal patterns by the language that you use on a regular basis, such as, "I am always".. "I never".. I could never".. etc For example, "I am always ignored", "Nobody ever listens to me", "This always happens to me", "I can never do it myself", are the examples of victim archetypal dialogue.

As described in Caroline Myss's best selling book *Sacred Contracts,* certain archetypes play a more prominent role in each of our lives, but everyone shares four of these, which she calls survival archetypes: *Child, Prostitute, Saboteur and Victim.*

There are many ways to describe archetypes, but we think the best way is by viewing oneself as a tapestry of emotional circuits and transitional moods, actions, reactions, and general patterns of behaviour.

Shakespeare said:
> *"All the world's a stage,*
> *And all the men and women merely players.*
> *They have their exits and their entrances;*
> *And one man in his time plays many parts,*
> *His acts being seven ages."*
>
> "As You Like It" (2.7.143-7)

It helps to think in terms of ourselves being able to act differently at different times or on different cues. As we go through life, we experience challenges, misfortunes, victories, and triumphs, and not all of us react and respond in the same exact way. We are all different based on our archetypal structure, and the archetypes that are more dominant in our personality.

Understanding archetypes can be a magnificent journey of self-exploration and it can play an important part in how we interact with people. We learn to be more compassionate, understanding and tolerant of ourselves and others. We come face to face with the blocks that prevent us from being our true selves. We learn to stop judging and to become more accepting of people.

While exploring archetypes, it is important to see each one in terms of three specific aspects: one is neutral, one is shadow, and one is light. All three parts are of equal importance. If you focus too much on one aspect there is a possibility that you will miss the learning and become engrossed in a superficial feeling of your own self importance. Although that may sound harsh, it is possible because it happened to our client Claire. As soon as she discovered she had a Victim archetype, she thought that she had found the Holy Grail. She could now label her unhappiness! This is not the smartest thing to do, as the more you focus on one thing, the more you will experience it.

Neutral
All the archetypes are essentially neutral, but each has a light and a shadow aspect.. 'Neutral' implies neither good nor bad. It is non-consequential. Basically, a victim is just doing the best that he or she can with their level of understanding at the time. Victims never intend harm to themselves or anyone else and they just bob along in life. Often they are oblivious to their patterns of behaviour and never see the need to change. For example, when there is conflict or discord, the victim will always assume the problem is with the other person, never him or herself.

Shadow

'Shadow' implies that there are subconscious motivations for acting as the victim. For example, victims usually get more attention, sympathy, and understanding. They rarely feel the need to initiate behavioural changes for themselves. People generally accept victim-type behaviour, because the victim's life history can be so profound. Victims can evoke sympathy, such that others are sometimes convinced of their plight, feel immense sympathy for them, and would find it heartless to demand personal changes from them.

Light

'Light' implies the illumination of behavioural patterns that keep people stuck in their own unhappiness. Once recognised, that pattern can be changed, preferably in a 'non-judgemental' way. Patience and understanding of self are important here. When the behavioural pattern has changed, the need for constant sympathy, understanding and attention is no longer there. This is like a 'rite of passage' into maturity.

According to Carl Jung, the Shadow aspect in our archetypal makeup is very common and reflects deeper elements of our psyche. It also reflects a part of us that has become separated or disconnected during our younger years of development. By its very name, the shadow conjures up images of the unknown, dark, mysterious and often troubling dimensions of our personality. Because they are unacceptable to our conscious mind, we tend to sweep them under the rug, to keep them in the dark.

By comparison, the opposite side to the *shadow* is the *light*, which embraces self expression rather than chaos and careless behaviour. Instead of only focusing on the shadow, you should also welcome the glow and brilliance that awaits you in the 'light'. The shadow doesn't seem to have a conscience or, if so, chooses not to use it. Our *shadow* may appear in dreams, and desires, often recognised as someone who is bad or wrong and despicable - always someone to be frightened or ashamed of.

The *shadow* behaviour can be recognised in falsehoods; telling untruths about yourself or others, malicious gossiping and/or pretending to be someone you are not. It is also found in dysfunctional relationships and friendships; manipulating others to do and to be what you want. Threatening or aggressive behaviour is a recognisable trait, as it tries to dominate and bully others into a particular way of thinking or behaving. The *shadow* is an aspect of the subconscious that may reveal deeper thoughts and fears as experienced in dreams and fantasies. It can also take on direct physical form when one is confused, drunk, drugged or feeling betrayed.

As read and discussed widely in the self-development archives and forums, the *shadow*-self is described as the ego, or as the frightened or fearful self. This frightened element is the part of ourselves that is afraid to be loved wholly; wanted and loved for who we are, not for "what" we are or the image we present to the world. The *shadow* self is panicky and anxious and is constantly creating or seeking problematic situations and/or chaos. This can be done consciously or subconsciously.

In spiritual terminology the *shadow* can be referred to as the "Fragmented Spirit". It is written that, during our formative years, we endure emotional trauma, separation or rejection etc. The spirit becomes frightened and fragmented. We then generally spend most of our lives trying to re-establish our sense of self (self-esteem) and to feel "whole again"! Many psychotherapeutic methods, spiritual paths, and religious dogmas are dedicated to self-discovery, spirit re-integration, and soul retrieval.

Something will eventually happen in your life to stir up these archetypes within you and wake you up to old and limiting behavioural patterns that no longer serve you. These triggering events may include life threatening illness, divorce, and loss or betrayal of any kind. Faced with a strong and urgent need to take care of yourself in a way that you never did before, consciously or unconsciously you begin to challenge the four survival archetypes.

The Victim

How many times have people tried to help you improve your life by being honest with you about your behaviour, yet you defend that behaviour as though it was your last crust of bread? Try not to be shy about admitting this to yourself, because as soon as you get over the shock that people see you in a way that you try desperately hard to hide, then your life can truly begin to change for the better. No shame or judgement is associated with any of these archetypes, because they have assisted you in coping with life's pressures, rejections and loss. The earth spins between seven hundred to nine hundred miles per hour in a twenty-four-hour period, unless, of course, you live on the North Pole where the earth spins at zero miles per hour. The planet earth does not stay in one place all the time; similarly, we too must move along with it and evolve unless we want to stay frozen over and in the complete darkness of eternal night.

There comes that time in everyone's life when change is inevitable. You will know when that time is for you. You will need to take action; chip away or demolish old habits and begin to reconstruct yourself.

The Saboteur

When we observe others and ourselves there are events that might seem regrettable. There are times that if you had the chance again you might do things differently and just go for it. The beauty of hindsight, you may say. However in looking at these times there are justifiable reasons why things happened as they did;

Sometimes it is due to just not believing in yourself and that you truly deserve the best.

Other people can do it but not me.. The saboteur archetype exists in all of us and can be critically destructive if not kept under control and halted.

"I will lose everything", "it will never work" or "I will do it another time". Generally, the *saboteur* is an archetype that symbolises the way we interrupt and terminate the process of maturity and personal development. The saboteur does not seize the moment and run with it. The saboteur does not focus on the positive or preferred outcome. Instead the *saboteur* archetype looks for ways to procrastinate and/or avoid said outcome.

The Prostitute

When one thinks of a 'prostitute', images of the red light district, disadvantaged women, drug addiction and pimps might come to mind. However in the language of archetypes a prostitute is one who gives much of herself for little in return.

A prostitute is one who undervalues herself and is in emotional deficit and crisis.

For example think of people you know who are always there to help out in any situation, at the other end of the phone; available to listen to endless sorrows of unhappiness. This archetypal feature is recognisable in one who seems worn out physically and emotionally and is of either sex.

As a result, the language of the prostitute is "What is in this for me?"; "If I do this then what will I get in return?" This archetype is always negotiating interactions with people in terms of profit or loss. The *prostitute* tries to hold control and rarely engages in or maintains healthy long-term relationships.

The Wounded Child

The wounded *child* holds onto memories and traumas from the past. This archetype finds it difficult to mature because of the "wound or weight" it carries around on its back. It relates everything to the past, cannot, and is sometimes unwilling to look into or face the future as a mature adult. "Who will take care of me?", "I can never go there on my own", "Will you come with me? ", "I can never do that on my own", "It's too hard for me", etc.

To paraphrase the words of John F. Kennedy, "Ask not what others can do for you to make your life better, instead ask what you can do to make their lives better". Embrace these words into your own personal life.

Some introspective questions to ponder;
Ask yourself, do you barter or trade off your vital energy in the stock exchange of life?

Yes [ ] No [ ]

If so, how?

....
....
....
....
....

Are you capable of taking all that you have experienced as a child and becoming a responsible adult? Yes [ ] No [ ]

If so, how?

....
....
....
....
....

In this chapter, as we introduce you to your archetypes you will have a choice on how to interpret them for yourself. The purpose of this is for you to become more aware of your personality traits and to be understanding of others. Everyone has many aspects to their personality. Sometimes we can dwell on the least favourable aspect of ourselves. Sometimes we fail to recognise the archetype that holds us back from being our authentic self. How easy is it to hear that you enact the Victim archetype on a regular basis? This is your means of controlling people and circumstances around you. Perhaps you are constantly sabotaging yourself to succeed personally or professionally. There are probably times in your life that you would love to express the artist in you, or the actor or the writer. If this is the case, then we ask you to make a note of it, because this will help you to become more of your authentic self. Some archetypal patterns or personality types may frighten you. Perhaps you are intimidated, and avoid them. We ask you to identify this and work on methods to help deal with them that will help improve your self-esteem. The more we avoid that, which we are afraid of, the stronger the fear will remain a threat to us. In the following discussion of archetypes we have included movies and the main actors therein, to will help you identify dominant and individual archetypal patterns.

Keep in mind that the purpose of working on archetypes is to not dwell on the negative aspect of the archetype, but rather to focus on the illumination of the *shadow*. Take for example the victim archetype. It is loaded with "woe is me" "why, why, why?" internal and external language. The victim really wants power, and has a deep yearning desire to be free to effectuate and externalise self-esteem of the highest and most honourable kind. After night there comes the day; after sun down there is sunrise; with despair there is hope. Every shadow has its light aspect, and with archetypes there is the glow and brilliance that awaits you. This is the beam of light that shines from your true self. Have fun with this discovery, try not to internalise and analyse the information too much. Remain conscious of the questions you pose to yourself. Begin your question with "how", not "why", and "what", not "where". *How* can I make this happen, *what* steps do I need to take, *what* habits do I need to invoke and *how* do I reward myself for these efforts?

Here is a list of archetypes to choose from, but by all means discover and make up some of your own:

Choose archetypes that you feel best suit your personality. Stay open-minded and curious.

....
....
....
....
....

Choose the archetypes that you would like to see expressed in a more profound way in your personality e.g. the Goddess, Artist, Networker, King etc

....
....
....
....
....

Identify the Archetypes that frighten you or threaten you in some way or rather the archetypes that you loathe in others e.g. Thief, Vampire, Trickster etc

....
....
....
....
....

The Warrior

Noble defender who acts with honour even if he doesn't fully believe in the cause. He fights for the cause and will do so till his death. He has noble qualities and he always sticks up for the underdog. He is a leader (or a follower) and definitely a man's man, or a G.I. Jane!

Shadow: He thinks that his beliefs are the ultimate virtue and sole purpose of himself. He is unwavering in the consistency of his chosen belief system. He perceives everything as black and white, and he will not countenance any compromise. There is no room for commonsense in his world-view. When he considers it necessary he is quite capable of killing the underdog too. He is a fighter and can be seen as a protector. He can make for a loyal body guard or assassin

Light: The warrior fights for others. His deepest and most heartfelt desire would be to defend his own cause.

Example: Arnold Schwarzenegger in "Terminator", Clint Eastwood in "Dirty Harry", Russell Crowe in "Gladiator", Brad Pitt in "Seven". Kevin Costner in "The Bodyguard"

The Knight

Today the Knight can be recognised as a cavalier, escort, aristocrat or gentleman. A noble partisan, he acts with honour and is a man of the highest calibre. The Knight holds his shield over his heart. He is protective of himself and of others. According to Caroline Myss "unlike mythical images he has no wish to rescue the lady or damsel in distress, rather be rescued by the woman who can remove the shield that protects his heart. This will not be a fair maiden but a strong and empowered woman who knows her own mind."

Shadow: He doesn't let his heartache or physical pain control him but he rises above adversity. He maintains a dignified composure. He is phlegmatic, pensive and he can suffer in silence. He maintains that adversity is character-building and essential to his value system. He believes in romance and longs, but waits patiently for his lady love. Every Knight must have a quest, but for some knights, the quest is unattainable (e.g. The Holy Grail).

Light: His openness and vulnerability, when expressed, is genuine, honest and often deeply profound. It is not self-serving. He does not wrap himself in the cloak of self pity and victimhood. He is the fearless leader and loyal to the core. He truly is the knight in shining armour and reflects the light rather than the shadow, illuminating honesty, loyalty, trust and undying love. He is noble in the face of adversity.

Movie Examples: Viggo Mortensen in "The Return of the King", Alec Guinness/Ewen Mc Gregor as Obi-Wan Kenobi in "Star Wars", Sean Connery in "First Knight", and Errol Flynn in "Robin Hood", Clark Gable as Johnny in "Somewhere I'll Find You"

The Best Friend: (Companion):
This person is sweet, safe and unpretentious. He will never let anyone down if he can help it. He is the noble trustee of his friends. He is responsible and decent, and generously gives his time to his friends. He never judges or criticises, and jests at shortcomings and out–of-character behaviour like getting drunk at parties and singing karaoke out of key. He is a genuine person and a regular Mr. Nice Guy. This man or woman is generally non-confrontational and would feel hurt and pain before ever hurting another person's feelings. Friendship is one of his or her highest values.

Shadow: Can get walked over by careless and overpowering personalities. He can often be misunderstood. Has the desire to be in control and always thinks things through. He has a tendency to place others before himself.

Light: Genuine self-belief and enduring self-acknowledgement.

Movie Examples: Jimmy Stewart in "It's a Wonderful Life", Hugh Grant in "Four Weddings and a Funeral", Kevin Spacey in "American Beauty"

The Boss:

The boss has been historically a man but over the last century women have assumed this role with fervour. Although a commendable achiever and a success on many levels, this woman is a high flyer and never takes no for an answer. She will walk over anyone to get to the top of her success ladder. Never a woman to lurk around the water cooler to gossip, she despises layabouts and slow-thinking individuals. She doesn't generally earn respect but almost always demands it. Her professional success is her highest reward and material possessions are symbolic of her self worth.

Shadow: Sad and lonely, she has excellent social skills but is short on courtesy and genuine graces. She can be non-diplomatic and rude. Full of unresolved childhood wounds, she probably drinks strong liquor and enjoys the company of males where she feels accepted. She certainly does not feel obliged to discuss feelings or emotional issues. She feels safe in men's company.

Light: Self-esteem and acceptance of herself and others, makes the boss a natural leader. She may be charismatic and inspirational. As she works through her shadow, she can look forward to a greater sense of self-worth and self-esteem. She may even discover that she has time to hang out at the water cooler and idly chat, because she now has nothing to prove or lose.

Movie Examples: Meryl Streep in "The Devil wears Prada", Annette Bening in "American Beauty", and Cate Blanchett in "Elizabeth", Joan Crawford in "Best Of Everything", Bette Davis in "June Bride"

The Nurturer:

This lady is generally full of emotion, and capable. She is trust-worthy and focuses on the good in all people. She nourishes the body, mind and spirit. She is not your typical Mrs. Beaten or Suzy Homemaker but embraces people graciously. This woman can take care of everyone. She listens attentively and is a pleas-ure to have around. She can see the needs within others and feels compelled to reach out. She longs to touch the hand or the shoulder of the heavily laden one.

Shadow: The shadow nurturer experiences a hollow emptiness in-side, and uses nurturance as a way to make others indebted to her (as in Smother Mother). She silently longs for the care and love that she extends to be reciprocated. She is often used by others and can be taken for a soft touch. She wounds easily and heals slowly.

Light: As this archetype illuminates, she develops genuine self-es-teem and a strong belief in herself. This will bring an unwavering, rooted sense of self. She is destined to love and approve of herself.

Movie Examples: Robin Williams in "Mrs. Doubtfire", Jennifer Connelly in "A Beautiful Mind", and Julie Andrews in "Mary Poppins"

The Crusader:

Is a dedicated fighter and advocate. This archetype can be of either sex so keep in mind if you are male to look for similar signs in yourself. She is a business-woman who rarely misses deadlines and who always gets the job done. She can be described as a woman wearing a man's suit. This lady will just about walk over anyone who gets in her way. She rarely displays the need for a partner or a husband unless it is to pump fuel in her car, change a tire or please her in bed. She is ultimately headstrong and single-minded and has little time for those who are emotional or needy. Any opposition is considered a challenge to which she is equal.

Shadow: She is lonely beyond words. As her archetypal behaviour suggests she is a woman in mans clothing. Going against her true nature her heart is normally blocked and she will suffer for the loss of true love and companionship. Physically she could suffer with pre-menstrual tension and headaches, and could easily get chest pain and heart burn.

Light: Longing to exhibit her vulnerable side, she is an excellent mother once she releases her need to control, and surrenders to her feminine side. Her life changes for the better. Her hard exterior starts to melt and her interior begins to shine through, full of generous acceptance and love of herself and for others. She has self-esteem and soon she will feel genuine, grounded and alive.

Movie Examples: Joan Collins in "Dynasty", Courtney Cox in "Dirt", Demi Moore in "Disclosure"

The Free Spirit:

She is the eternal optimist and you can often find her floating through the garden or dancing in the kitchen. She loves nature colours, creatures and sounds. She speaks softly and sweetly. She wears her heart on her sleeve and is miffed at how people can be harsh and/or unkind. She generally wears feminine and almost childlike costumes or clothing. Often playful and airheadish, she hums and sings to her heart's content. Rarely frowning, she smiles although she can cry easily, but not for long as she is quickly restored to full joy by the sight of a falling star or the wings of a butterfly. She follows her heart and rarely her head and can be heard saying "Isn't it just lovely"?

Shadow; Never streetwise and always immature, she can be subjected to being used and treated badly. She usually needs protection from predators and bullies.

Light: Strong and self-assured, this archetype can be a leader, crusader and teacher.

Movie Examples: Lucille Ball in "I Love Lucy", and "Donkey (Eddie Murphy)" in Shrek

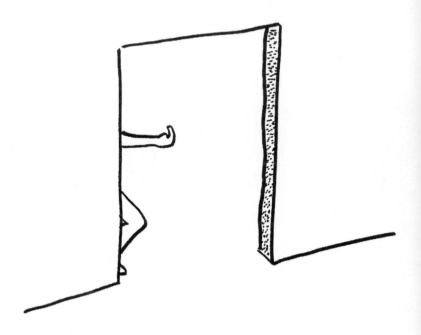

The Seductress:

This woman is mature and wise to the world. She can hold court and is usually the centre of attention. She flirts openly and sometimes dangerously. Men are smitten and dazzled by this woman. Often feeling under a spell, men can be easily taken in by her charms, marry in haste and then repent at leisure. As part of her alluring behaviour, she is generally despised by other women and rarely holds onto female companions and friends. This is usually because women recognise women's behaviour sooner and more accurately than men do. She can also size people up very quickly and get a handle on everyone in a room, the minute she enters. She is the ultimate survivor.

Shadow: Mysterious and manipulative, cynicism guides everything she says or does. She only attracts a certain type of man. Lonely and disconnected to other people's feelings and emotions, she is driven by the hardness of "the tough broad". Prone to broken and dysfunctional relationships, she rarely has the comfort of a steadfast companion. She is manipulative and cynical. She must have her own way, regardless of who she hurts.

Light: Self-esteem, compassion and vulnerability

Movie Examples: Bette Davis in "Jezebel", Vivienne Leigh in "Gone with the wind" and Sharon Stone in "Basic Instinct".

Lost Soul:

This archetype is a sensitive being, always understanding and terribly tortured within. This is a man or woman who is characteristically searching for him- or herself. Unable to find peace (s)he keeps looking and rarely settles for one relationship or finds contentment in any given place to live. Lost souls may find themselves joining cults, groups or religious organisations to feel connection and a sense of acceptance. This person is vulnerable and highly suggestible. Outward appearances may suggest strength and self-confidence, but inwardly they are looking for themselves and they experience tremendous torment. They are wanderers and feel like outcasts. In work they can be creative, but also loners.

Shadow: This archetype is secretive, brooding, passive aggressive and unforgiving. Invariably, they are in long term anguish. They cause unbearable torment to those who care about them.

Light: Self-assured and self-confident, open and inviting. Once this person begins to work through the shadow aspect of their personality, self-worthiness and self-esteem emerge. Oftentimes they can become a teacher and writer, or healer

Movie Example: Mel Gibson in "Lethal Weapon", Ron Perlman as Beast in "Beauty and the Beast", Shrek, (Mike Myers) in "Shrek", Alan Ladd as "Shane"

Equal Opportunity Slut:

This archetype can be of either sex and can easily be recognised among young women and gay men. They look for friendship, comfort and love wherever he or she can find it. They dress up in seductive, revealing clothing and attract anyone who takes them up on their offers. If a woman, her likely candidates are men, but she will succumb to the desires of women also. With the belief that they have a free spirit and that "it is just the way they are", they are living an illusion. Wounded from within this archetype learns to associate attention and acceptance only from sexual interludes and encounters. She often resorts to prostitution and succumbs to addiction. This archetype could have a history of abuse and parental rejection. With increased low self-esteem and severe low self-worth, this person is in denial of inner needs and a troubled past. Rarely able to maintain lasting relationships, (s)he has childlike tendencies and is often in search of someone to look after her.

Shadow: Fabricates the truth and lives in a fantasy world. This person cannot be trusted or relied upon. With extreme low self-worth, she has little value for loyalty and will experience depression and sleepless nights.

Light: Pure self-esteem and self-worth. They can be excellent with children and often times will become a crusader for women's rights and an advocate for victimised children.

Movie Example: Julia Roberts in "Pretty Woman" and "Erin Brockovich", Charlize Theron in "Monster" and Richard Gere in "American Gigolo"

Dumb Blonde:

Both sexes fall into this archetypal category. Easily recognised by external dialog like "I don't quite understand what you mean" or "What does that mean?" or "I don't get it". They generally try to keep their life as simple and as uncomplicated as possible. They focus on their physical appearance and material possessions. They have a terrific sense of humour and often find amusement in situations where others can't.

Shadow: Although well-disguised, this archetypal character has low self-esteem and is prone to addiction such as overspending, alcohol and drug abuse. They also find it difficult to cope with mid-life and ageing in general and will suffer bouts of depression. They generally feel angry on the inside, but rarely express their inner fears and needs. In fact they are out of touch with who they truly are. They get tired of the ridicule but find it difficult to change and to be otherwise taken seriously. This person can be used and abused by others.

Light: Within the Dumb Blonde is a highly intelligent person who has genuine desires to excel in educational and academic achievements and to be openly recognised for it. They have strong hopes to be equally acknowledged for their genuine passion and maternal instincts. Their illumination is their self-esteem and self-love.

Movie Examples: Marilyn Monroe in "Some Like it Hot", "Reese Weatherspoon in "Legally Blonde" 1 & 2. Melanie Griffith in "Working Girl"

SNIFF

Grim Weeper:

This archetype lives and breeds off bad news of any kind. Of either sex, this person has hardly a positive thought in their head. Their "social currency" is doom and gloom. The last thing that they would ever want is to have happy thoughts or even to articulate them. This person reads up on illnesses and disease and will never miss reading the obituary column and/or news on the hour. Often confused with the "Gossip" this archetype rarely looks for any kind of joy but always finds doom and gloom wherever they go.

Shadow: This archetype can often suffer with various types of airborne illnesses, like colds, flue's, general aches and pains and of course everyone will know about what ails them. Suspicious and paranoid, they are angry and suffer with isolation and depression. They are fussy eaters and have a tendency to drink alone, so alcoholism, outbursts of anger, and poverty are common. They tend to have a logical outlook on life and are out of touch with their creative side. They are in denial of their need to be wanted and loved.

Light: The illumination of this archetype is joy. Along with joy this person needs to get in touch with his or her own unique self. This includes their qualities of positivity, lightness, grace and peace. They need to feel peace and relaxation. This will lead to self-worth and self-esteem. This archetype longs to love and nurture others as well as receiving fully and feeling the love and nurturing from others too. They secretly hope for someone to brighten up their day and they are craving to have a positive outlook on life. They can be excellent with children and have a playful side that is bursting to shine through.

Walter Matthau in "Grumpy old Men", Alastair Sim as Ebenezer Scrooge in "A Christmas Carol" and Margaret Hamilton as the witch in "The Wizard of Oz"

The Itinerant [Wanderer]:

This archetype can be of either sex and is easy to recognise. He comes here, he goes there and he travels everywhere. Unlike the free spirit, this archetype has gypsy and traveller like qualities. He enjoys new ventures, discovering new things and being thoroughly captivated and enchanted by variety. He is creative and easily stimulated by different people, places and especially new beginnings. He has always been happy to be on his own and manages well.

Shadow: The shadow of this archetype is one of solitude and detachment. He has a restless spirit and a tender view of his transient ways. In search of that special dwelling to call his own, he lives in the moment. He reluctantly attaches himself to anyone or thing. His expectations of security are undefined and he has an underlying and hidden fear of feeling obliged to leave, not belonging or not being wanted around. Unfortunately it can, and often does, become a self-fulfilling prophecy.

Light: He has an optimistic outlook which in turn illuminates even more when he settles down and accepts himself for who he is. He subconsciously desires a reason or purpose to stay in one place and when he finds it, his heart soars as he finally discovers the treasured home within himself. The realisation that he "doesn't have to go anywhere" or "leave anyone at anytime" balances the itinerant archetype.

Movies: Judy Garland in "The Wizard of Oz", David Janssen and Harrison Ford in "The Fugitive" and Bill Bixby in "The Incredible Hulk"

"Once you are real you cannot become unreal again".

Task:

Make a list of the strategies you intend to follow through with regarding your own archetypal illumination:

....
....
....
....
....

For the next seven days I invoke to: ....
....
....
....
....
....

My daily practice today is:

....
....
....
....
....

Affirmation: I embrace all new and desired transformations in my life

Section 5

RELATIONSHIPS

"The quality of your life is the quality of your relationships."
Anthony Robbins

☺

Life is all about relationships of one kind or another and there are many kinds of relationships. We are constantly relating to people, animals, places or things. In the beginning we form a relationship with our mother, then our father, siblings, friends, teachers, employers, girlfriends, partners, husband or wife.

There are different types of relationships. For instance people develop bonding relationships with friends, enrapturing relationships with lovers, nurturing relationships with children and parents, comforting relationships with pets and possessive relationships with car's, careers, houses and boats etc.

Obviously we live in changing times where people face difficulties in dealing with interpersonal complexities whilst sustaining the uncertainty of relationship survival. Without question, there will always be challenges in relationships and if you think not, then you are living in "never-never land" with Pollyanna and Peter Pan.

Books, prose, poetry and music are inspired by, and inspire the joy and pain of relationships – so what's the magic potion vital in maintaining and enhancing a lasting and loving relationship? Sustain a hot bod, pump and stretch your skin so that you are forever twenty something, get a boob job, have an incredible career, short skirt and high heels? Men must stay in shape, look like movie stars or rock jocks, adore the ground she walks on, be in touch with their feminine side, be CEO's or something equivalent, have a fabulous house and drive a super car. Nothing less than highly intelligent, extremely successful, a house in the country and a fat bank account is acceptable. Everything else is an added bonus. Did we mention love...? Oh well, an extravagant and exorbitant wedding should suffice.

Joking aside, once together, there are certain personality aspects, or archetypal patterns (which you are familiar with by now) that will cause problems within the most nurturing and loving relationship. Three of these patterns are "neediness" "criticism" and "jealousy".

NEEDINESS

Neediness must not be confused with communicating your needs to your partner. Neediness is insisting on their constant reassurance and validation.

Criticism is not letting other people be themselves, regardless of how awful their faults may seem to you. Remember they have to live with themselves too, and their faults could be the very thing that keeps them sane or happy. If you don't like their habits, and they won't change, then it might be better to find someone new and try changing them instead.

CRITICISM

Jealousy is another way of saying "I am not good enough and I am afraid that he/she will want somebody else instead of me". It's a risk you take isn't it? The truth is, is that there will always be someone better looking, smarter, richer, more popular and sexier than you, but so what? If they want them, then, let them go! You are jealous because you don't believe in your own self worth. Get working on your self-esteem otherwise you will lose your partner for sure.

JEALOUSY

"Never idealise others. They will never live up to your expectations. Don't over-analyse your relationships. Stop playing games. A growing relationship can only be nurtured by genuineness."

Leo F. Buscaglia

It is normal, as individuals, to experience varying degrees of insecurity in our lives, but it is how we deal with these insecurities that really count and makes the difference. If you are bored in your life; and if you need more entertainment or attention and your partner is "it", then maybe you are being a little bit too unreasonable here. After all, if you want a circus act, go to the circus!! If you want a normal relationship temper your expectations! In fact, some relationships are so volatile that they resemble a circus. Many people in these relationships wish they could run away and join an orphanage...

RUNNING AWAY TO THE ORPHANAGE

On a more serious note: if you are truly at the end of your tether and you are frustrated beyond words, well this could be a sign that there are cracks and/or deeper problems in your relationship which you are avoiding. You will have to approach this sooner or later. A good question to ask yourself from time to time is:

"What, if anything in my relationship am I not facing"?

Write it down:

....
....
....
....
....

What steps can I take to improve this situation?

....
....
....
....
....

What if anything in my relationship do I like?

....
....
....
....
....

Something to keep in mind: You don't want your partner to be a carbon copy of yourself. You are meant to be different, so allow each other to be different! Of course, where necessary, you will need to discuss, and communicate your feelings, fears and concerns regarding the dynamics, stability and future of your relationship, but for goodness sake, keep it real!

We both give credence to the theory that we are here to learn how to love each other and ourselves. This implies learning to go it alone, be independent, self sufficient, self-reliant and emotionally fit. You must take yourself to the next best level of your life without insisting that you have to have that man or woman to make it happen for you. (Keep it in perspective. They are the icing on the cake - if you are lucky enough to find the right icing!) In this way you are sure to be a positive influence on other people's lives as well as on your own, without being false or re-inventing sainthood.

The objective in relationships is to respect and get along with each other regardless of who the other is; a family member, friend, colleague or lover. This involves a genuine desire to be of indisputable benefit to one another. Obviously, this does not mean that you should be a doormat or a "Ninny Hammer". On the contrary this involves primarily a self-respecting relationship with yourself; understanding and honouring your own emotional and physical needs, limitations and boundaries. This way, when you are in a relationship of any kind, you have increased flexibility in your thinking, are more grounded, and have a greater capacity to understand and appreciate yourself and the other person. There is little debate when it comes to developing self-esteem, it is a life long journey and responsibility. This journey requires self–awareness, less "junk talk" and a flurry of positivity with a starburst of trials, errors and triumphs!

LOW SELF ESTEEM

You are your own responsibility, which literally means that you are 'able-to- respond', make choices and decisions about what you want and what you are not prepared to settle for! If you think that all you need to make your life perfect is a particular type of woman or dream man, think again. That is similar to thinking that if you move to a different house, or another country, or even get a new wardrobe/face lift, your life will be "perfect" (apart from looking like a Siamese cat!). You will definitely feel a change and may feel up-beat for a while, but it is temporary. To create permanent change you can only change yourself. How would you like it, if someone tried to change you? It might not feel very pleasant. We don't want to sound pessimistic in any way. A friend, partner and/or lover can enhance your life but they are not responsible for your inner peace and happiness. That is your job!

Some hints for you!

Do not neglect your relationship and never threaten the security of the relationship.
Be respectful towards each other and avoid making snide remarks or taking pot-shots that undermine the other ~ it's not classy or nice.
Arrange time to discuss your differences. Just because you have difficulties with each other doesn't mean you have to blurt out your malevolence just when they've burnt dinner again, or when you are on your third glass of wine.
Tell each other what your needs are and get some kind of commitment to make good-hearted behavioural changes.
Focus on your partner's qualities and what is working in your relationship, and why it feels great to be with them.
Never dismiss the other persons concerns.
Listen and pay attention to their likes and dislikes.
Be spontaneous in the bedroom and anywhere else!
Give each other space.

Devote at least one night a week with each other without distraction – no phones, kids, mothers in law, pets etc
Tell him or her "I love you" last thing at night and first thing in the morning. And mean it!!
Lighten up!

We haven't written anything about families with children because we know nothing about that… Sorry! ☺

> *"Why can't we get all the people together in the world that we really like and then just stay together? I guess that wouldn't work. Someone would leave. Someone always leaves and then we have to say good-bye. I hate good-byes. I know what I need. I need more hellos"*
>
> Charlie Brown

Loving and leaving

Sometimes love hurts and sadly that is part of what 'love is'. Love is "having to say good bye". We live in a duality of shadow and illumination, night and day, good and bad, negative and positive and, of course encounters and infatuations of being 'in love and 'out of love'. Falling in love can be described, as a form of madness, breaking up is also a form of madness, given the feelings that ensue. Both are extreme emotions, neither being bad but equally as intoxicating. Falling in love requires a sense of balance and control (and yet you can feel wildly out of control at times).

A relationship break up will require extra self-care, depending on its impact and feelings of rejection. It's good to keep in mind that break ups can often bring up old hurts and rejections from your past that still need healing. So a break-up can require a lot more reparation than you think.

When you first fall in love you are so full of emotions, that it feels as though a high voltage current is running through you.

Energy is at an all time high and you feel on top of your world. You romanticise and fantasise. There is the anticipation of all kinds of possibilities and you feel a lightness that has been often described as "walking on air" Then when the break up comes along, as it sometimes does, it feels as though your electricity is cut off. You have little to no energy and you feel as if you are at the bottom of your world. You feel as though your future has been stolen from you by a thief in the night. Your dreams and fantasies are gone and replaced by a sense of paralysis. The feelings of loss and sadness follow.

Biologically, the chemistry in your body is changing. There is less serotonin and adrenaline circulating through your brain. Your brain produces less endorphins and your heart rate slows. Less pheromones are produced and you experience bouts of depression.

That's when you need to get a "love support machine", and this is not the proverbial bottle-of-drowning-my-sorrows-in-a-top–shelf-tequila-or-beer. And, for goodness sake, don't think that by sleeping with the nearest guy or gal it is going to get you over your ex. By doing that, you will often feel even more emotionally empty and foolish than you did prior to the roll in the hay! Worse still – avoid launching yourself into the next and nearest relationship.

Once the crush is over, you may begin to recognise in your new relationship, many of the annoying nuances and insecurities that upset you in your previous relationship. For example you might find yourself playing those old tunes in your head over and over again, torturing yourself as you go.

Below you will find some of the old familiar tunes:

SAME OLD TUNES

"That means (s)he's not interested in me",
"(S)He is going to leave me",
"(S)He thinks I am weird",
"He hates my hair, my nose, my boobs, my hips, my bum etc",
"I knew that (s)he wasn't that interested in me anyway",
"Typical woman, she was only going out with me for my money",
"He was only using me for sex",
"He never called, that means he doesn't love me",
"He didn't buy me flowers that means he doesn't care",
"He is late again, that means he is taking me for granted",
"He is checking her out and that means he fancies her not me",
"He's so mean", "She's so selfish",
"He's so arrogant"; "She's so conceited"
"He never listens to how I feel", "I wonder what he is really thinking",
"I bet he never thinks about me that way"
"Who is he texting now, must pinch his phone and find out",
"I can't trust her; she's just like my ex-wife"
"She's always whining"…
"Cow", "Jerk" "I can't believe (s)he said that"
"Men!", "Women!"

When in a love relationship, deal with this internal dialog on your own or with a qualified therapist; don't expect your partner to solve your neurosis. This is clearly about your self-esteem or lack of it, not theirs.

If and when you realise that you are unhappy in a relationship you must seriously consider doing something about it. You will never get very far if you overprotect yourself, or the other person from the truth.

For instance some of the more common mistakes people make in relationships are:

- playing mind games;
- assuming that you know what the other is feeling or thinking;
- pretending that you don't care; telling untruths,
- creating minor jealousies and insecurities in the other;
- acting as if it doesn't bother you when it does;
- being macho
- hitting below the belt
- not being your real self.
- trying to make unreasonable changes in the other or yourself

Everyone is vulnerable and nobody wants to get hurt or seem foolish. The last thing anyone wants to hear or feel is rejection. You must be honest and say how you feel.

For example:

Talk to each other about your differences. If you are both seeking different things from each other then, you will have to face this. You will need to compromise, or move on and move out.

Do not interrupt the other and prevent him/her from speaking their mind

Don't assume that you know what they mean; ask them to explain

Be honest and deal with the truth not the fairy tale -"make believe" or fantasy that you may have conjured up.

Stop talking so much and listen occasionally..

Be kind

Get couple or individual counselling

Give yourselves plenty of space and time and in turbulent moments (as you're bound to have those) try not to threaten the relationship. It is just not a nice thing to do. Have some heart!

You will intuitively know when it's over. When that time comes around; go, quit, leave, exit, pack your stuff and run.

Do it! In time (and if possible) renew your friendship.

Remember that you will save time and further unhappiness for both of you by not hanging in there especially when you know its over. Listen to your intuition!

"Yesterday I was a dog. Today I'm a dog. Tomorrow I'll probably still be a dog. Sigh! There's so little hope for advancement".

Snoopy

LOVE SUPPORT MACHINE

Anyway let's get back to your "love support machine", the function of which is to restore your physical and emotional energy and well being. Getting over someone requires a plan. Remember that failing to plan is a plan to fail! Ugh! That sounds pat, but it happens to be true. You must become a "crusader" and have a step by step approach in order to nurture and love yourself. This will help you get over the person who probably wasn't right for you anyway.

Things to think about (and put into action):

- Don't get bitter; don't get even; *get smart.*
- Keep the door to your heart open
- Make sure you don't frighten yourself and others with your drama, sorrow and pain.
- Don't deny how you feel but work through it. Embrace your own personal space and freedom.

Feelings change; that is something you can count on. Remember your heart is not *actually* broken. You don't have to suffer endlessly. There is always a beginning, middle and an end to everything. Begin a new love affair with yourself. Learn to appreciate yourself in a way you may never have done before. Try not to give yourself a time limit to getting over him or her. Be your own personal love coach and take one day at a time. Watch comedy programmes and DVD's until things start to ease a little. Have a party and appear to be happy! Practice makes perfect!

WATCH COMEDY SHOWS ON T.V.

Some hints for you:

Acknowledge your feelings. Discuss how you feel with a trusted friend or counsellor

Keep to your normal routine. For example if you have always made your bed in the mornings, make sure to keep that up. If you have always taken the dog for a walk at certain times, well, keep doing that. Keep going to work; continue with your gym or your Pilates. Empty the dishwasher, do the laundry, take out the trash and try doing some voluntary work to take your mind off yourself!

Eat regular meals and drink water. Drink alcohol moderately, or as little a possible. Although it seems that alcohol is relaxing, it is actually a depressant, and insomniac.

Stay in contact with your friends and if they can't handle your *"all over the place"* emotions maybe you should break up with them too, or snap out of the whining. Apart from that, keep up with your work and social commitments.

Keep a journal. Have a make over. Visit the elderly and if "they tell you that there are more fish in the sea", *believe*, and thank them!

When you are in your next relationship don't bore the new person to death with stories about your ex. That's just more drama! Try talking about your hobbies instead. Whatever you do ensure that you don't try to remodel yourself to suit your new partner. Be yourself, and if the relationship is meant for you, they will love you just as you are and if they don't; don't worry, just let go and move on! May we emphasise that there will be another loving relationship for you in the future so keep the hope alive.

TRY TALKING ABOUT YOUR
HOBBIES INSTEAD

"I'll go with you"
Charlie Brown

There is *requited* love; that feeling of oneness with another, when everything seems to 'feel' right. It matures, remains "comfortable" or fades away. One thing that we know for sure is that feelings never stay the same. Loving feelings can grow, become deeper, more intense and/or simply comfortable. You can never relive an exact feeling or emotion because it evaporates and it's over. You can recreate similar experiences but it is always a little different. That is when you start to learn from your emotions. Your new relationship is not the old one; a break up is not inevitable and should it happen, it is not a replica of your last or previous rejections in your life. Your next first day at college is not the same as your last first day at college. Your next new neighbour is not the same as your last cranky or twenty-four-hour-*drum- playing* neighbour. You must raise your expectations and remember, keep looking for what you want, not for what you don't want.

your last NEIGHBOUR

Then there is *unrequited* love: The guys and gals who are just not that keen on you, and are too polite or selfish to say so. How many times do the ladies fall for the cad, the bold or lost boy, and/or the unscrupulous married man? They believe almost everything he says and imagine they hear everything he doesn't say. "Your eyes are like moon beams", "your hair is lovely"; "I've never felt skin so soft before". "You're like a model - I can't believe how lucky I am!". How many times do you fall for "honestly I am leaving my wife, I just need more time". What he is actually saying is "Don't go yet, I am not ready to say good bye".

Ahh! Men ye can't live with them and it can be lonesome without them.

What is your definition of what a man should be? Do you have some conjured-up images of what a man should be like? A prince who wakes you out of a deep and meaningless sleep, just like in the fairy tale "Sleeping Beauty" or the infamous Knight in Shining Armour, who sweeps you off your feet as he dazzles you with his *fait de complis* or incredible tales of slaying dragons? How about the regular guy who just happens to be decent and honest and wouldn't harm anyone intentionally? I wonder, ladies, would you be happy with him or be forever looking over his shoulder, on the dance floor, or in a restaurant, in the hopes that there may be a better catch for you to reel in?

What do you think a woman should be like? Perhaps she should be a princess, forever gentle and softly spoken, with long flowing blond hair and the perfect supple, toned and flawless body? Perhaps she should be a Goddess, sensuous, seductive and mysterious; a 'little' minx or a diamond in the rough. Of course there is the maternal figure with the appropriate back ground and genetics to carry your children, with good child bearing hips. There is the girl next door with the proper education who can easily adjust herself to your way of life. Possibly, what you think a woman should be is all of the above. The fact is that while you can always find what you are looking for; make sure that you are realistic with your expectations. *Enjoy the quirkiness of imperfection.*

There are two sayings that come to mind: "You never know true happiness until it's gone" and "A woman is only beautiful when she is loved." Both we believe *can* be true, however try this small exercise:

Write down:
1. When are the times you tell yourself that you are unhappy with your mate?
E.g. in the morning, over dinner, after a telephone call, before or after a sleep over, on nights out etc

....
....
....
....
....

Identify moments that you tell yourself that you are happy with your mate?

....
....
....
....
....

Are you continually finding fault with the man / woman in your life?
Yes [ ] No [ ]

Do you blame him/her for your unhappiness?
Yes [ ] No [ ]

Are you addicted to highs and lows? In other words does commotion of this kind help create the passion in your relationship which otherwise would not exist?
Yes [ ] No [ ]

> *"It's not whether you win or lose, but how you place the blame"*
>
> Snoopy

It is common, especially among men to think that further fields are greener. In this case you believe that the better someone is out there, waiting to be captivated by your charm. If you convince yourself that the woman you are with is not good enough for you, then, she may well move on before you do. We are not suggesting that if you have a genuine incompatibility that you shouldn't address the situation in an impartial way. In fact we strongly advise that you do! Regardless of your circumstances, sometimes it can be helpful to take a look at other areas in your life that aren't perfect and make some realistic changes there. It's not surprising how these changes can benefit your relationships too. Perhaps you might need to consider stress management techniques and/or include a regular relaxation routine.

In like manner we refer to times in your relationship where it's necessary to unwind and be happy. Make some effort at enjoying the simplest of things because being happy is much better for you than being unhappy.

Curiously, people imagine love as being dreamy eyed or hot for passion, and don't often realise that being in a mutually loving relationship is comfortable, relaxing and affirming of who you are as a person.

(S)He loves me, (S)he loves me not!

What are some of the telltale signs of someone who doesn't feel the way you do? Actions can speak louder than words.

He says he will call you and he doesn't

She forgets your name

He loses your phone number

She ignores you or shows little interest in talking to you in company

He tells you not to have desert so that you can watch your weight

She flirts with other men in front of you

He inquires about the cute blond who hangs around with you

He asks more about your friends than he does about you

She picks arguments and fights with you for no particular reason

He never asks you out to somewhere special (just the two of you)... "meet me at a Pete's Pizza Place" doesn't quite cut it !!

(S)he doesn't listen to much of what you say

(S)He doesn't share deeper fears and feelings with you

She mistakes you for your brother under the mistletoe at Christmas.

He never pays for your meal and he'd rather read the dailies over breakfast than talk to you.

(S)He is irritated by things that you do or say

He doesn't stay the night at your place.

She de-mans you or visa versa and embarrasses you in company

(S)He rejects your affection and terms of endearment

(S)He takes advantage of your vulnerability

(S)He is insensitive to your needs

He leaves the party with another woman (or man)

She leaves the party with another man (or woman)

He doesn't outwardly show support if you're challenged

He never asks you on a special night out

She has to do all the running as though she were in the Grand National

He never laughs at your jokes

He slams the door in your face

He calls the cops and reports you as a stalker

She tells you that she wishes that you were somebody else

He is dating you while trying to get back with his ex

She calls you in the middle of the night, locked out of her house and he says "Don't worry someone is bound to show up in the morning to let you in"

When she wants to talk, he says "can you hang on a minute until the game is over"

She asks "are you sure that you're not gay"?

S(He) gets a bogus emergency call during a dinner date and she/he has to leave.

He insists that you sweep the driveway, cut the grass and wash the cars on Saturday before you make breakfast

(S)He loves you just as a friend

He suggests that you go to the gym more often or get a new trainer

He doesn't want you to leave your things in his place

He leaves €100 on your night stand when leaving

She tells you that she's meeting her friends when she is seeing another guy

He asks you to go on a date with his friend

He doesn't respect you

She complains that "we never do anything fun; or you never take me here; there and everywhere!"

(S)He "stands you up" on a date

He stares at, or checks out other women when he is with you

She prefers to talk to your gold fish than converse with you

He flirts with other women in your company

There is always an excuse not to be with you. Excuses are like tiny rejections

He sees you as a fling or a good time girl

(S)He teases you but never commits

He says that he's not over his ex and/or that he is not looking for a relationship.

When your calls, texts and emails are rarely returned.

When you have to try too hard.

Remember don't get upset because he/she doesn't feel the same way about you. It's part of life and be grateful for what you have.

Think back to some of your past experiences and jot-down some notes so you don't re-enact or find yourself in a similar situation again.

....

....

....

....

....

Remember it is wonderful to get some respite from being single but for heaven's sake do not jeopardise your own self-worth and self-esteem by not reading the signs in time. Equally do not lead anyone "down the garden path" or mislead him or her in anyway because of your fears, needs or insecurities. Be honest with yourself and them! They may not find you irresistible at all, or they could be wildly attracted to you and want you more than you realise. Many people get into relationships just to escape being single. This is surely not the best foundation for an enduring relationship. Remember there is a man or woman out there somewhere for you, although the best relationship you will ever have is with yourself. Make that one work first!

Happy to be single

> *"Happiness is anyone and anything that's loved by you."*
> Charlie Brown

Let's take a look at the pleasures of being free and single. Where is it written that in order to be a complete person that your only benchmark is by maintaining a love relationship? It doesn't matter if it is dysfunctional, unhappy, dishonest or demoralising, or bad for your health. As long as you *have* a relationship well then you must be complete.... Not true! Don't settle with anyone just for the sake of having someone on your arm, or to keep you warm on cold nights, or even, dare we say, pay your bills. Instead know in advance the kind of person you wish to share your hopes and dreams with and patiently wait. Obviously you will need to be proactive in your quest but allow life to lead you there. "Patience can obtain many things".

Help! - I am not happy unless I am married NOW!

What about women who get frantic when they turn thirty-four? They go on a hunt to either marry the poor guy whom their dating: spike a guy's drink, (who discovers on awakening in a motel room that he has a ring on his finger!); Perchance - accidentally getting pregnant. If it can get worse than that; collapsing into a state of depression because you are not fulfilling your purpose as a woman. Correction ladies; surely that is only one of many purposes in your life as a female. Reproduction seems to be going out of fashion as careers and divorces are becoming more 'in vogue'. Women are having fewer children and later in their lives.

Nowadays when a woman considers getting pregnant or rather having a baby, and regardless of how much in love she is with *Mr. Right,* she had better be prepared to raise the child on her own; toute-seule, by herself. Look around you and notice how many single mothers there are, or married mums raising their children on their own. Familiarise yourself with how few of them are driving soft-top Merc's. Be wise ladies! It's not that easy -

Here are a few reasons why being single is a treasure. Contrary to various reports, being single can not only be good for your health, but it can also keep you sane and other people too.

Being single means you can:

Stay out all night without having to give excuses; explain where you have been and who you've been with

Partake in your own hobbies and pursuits as you please without judgement or whining

Stay up as late as you want

Leave the toilet seat up or down

Strip down an engine and leave the parts all over the dining room

Play your own style of music as loud as you like

Work as many hours as you want

Have your buddies over to drink beer and play cards

Eat from cartons and cans; then belch and fart loudly

Compare the size of your bellies

Make a mess and only clean up when you feel like it

Leave the dishes until morning

Stay in on a Friday night because you want to

Lie in on the weekends

Only watch movies or documentaries that you enjoy

Not have to watch soaps or reality TV

Wear what you want, when you want ☺

Read, or watch TV in the middle of the night

Maintain your wild side without reprieve

Really stretch out in your bed

Wear your fluffy bed socks or flannel P.J.'s to bed

Get out of going to their family gatherings on holidays and being nice to spoilt kids

Have your pillows, cushions, teddy's, toys, cats or dogs on your bed all night long

Watch a ball game; shout and roar as if you were in the jungle practising you're elephant mating call!

By the way from time to time men find it cute when a woman plays around like a little girl but in the real world a woman needs to act her age. Try not to be a "Baby Jane" when you are really an "Auntie Mame". The same applies to men; a woman really likes it when a man is in touch with his feminine side and has little difficulty in mopping up her tears, but please if you are a man then be yourself; roar once in a while and if you really must; leave the toilet seat up, even if it means that the ladies will fall to the bottom of the loo, high heels up in the air and curse the day that you were born!!

"Life is what happens when you're busy making other plans"

John Lennon

There may come a time to give your love life another chance and now could be the time. There is no way of knowing if you are making the "right" decision, but one thing you will know for certain is that you are taking a chance, a risk and that you are embracing uncertainty. It could feel as though you are lowering the drawbridge from your castle walls and either inviting in or walking out to be with the man or woman whose heart has entered yours. Although inundated by psychics, tarot card readers and well meaning and optimistic friends, there is no way of telling your future and no crystal ball can proclaim that you will live happily ever after.

This could be the "right" time to listen to your heart, have faith in yourself and the other, and relinquish your need to control the outcome, and allow whatever is meant to be, to be.

In life, love presents itself quite out of the blue, and oftentimes there is no warning. So what do you do; "say that there is no room in your inn", or welcome it as though it were Christmas and you get the gift that you always wanted and waited for. Unlike previous chapters there are no questions, tasks or lists here; instead there are captured moments, newer memories and dreams that really do come true! Fly your kite, sail your boat, and live your dream. Carpe Diem

RESOLVE YOUR EMOTIONS
"IT'S TIME TO GET CRACKING AND TO DO THE WORK"

Anger

Anger is a necessary emotion. Unfortunately, we have often learned, and/or been conditioned to never lose our temper or lose our cool. Showing or displaying this emotion is considered a bad thing. This is not necessarily so. When this emotion is suppressed, it's effects can be horrendous to all concerned.

Anger can be a direct result of too much stress. The body/mind will interpret stress as overwhelming. There is a need to release and let go. This can be recognised as loud and sudden bursts of anger or rage. We repeat that there are no good or bad emotions - just emotions... Simply put, too much anger is bad for your health and too little anger is equally harmful. It is commonly understood that anger is internalised depression. Harbouring hostility or resentment can lead to anger. Unexpressed anger can create other problems. For instance, passive aggressive behaviour implies that you can't say how you feel. Inadvertently, there is a strong inclination to sarcasm. It is a way in which you think that 'you are getting back at someone', without actually expressing how you really feel. Bullying tendencies can come along for the ride as a sure sign that you are unable to express your feelings and you fight to control the other, or situation or both.

Is anger an issue for you?

By taking a look at your life, your family and friends; you will be able to recognise patterns in your communication. For instance how did your mother/ father express their feelings, dislikes and disappointments? Have you inherited similar attitudes and behaviours? Have your friends ever commented on your reactions to events, or are they afraid of your wrath if they did? Sometimes we are the last to see ourselves in a negative way, but good friends will tell you if you ask them.

By completely controlling your outward behaviour, you are internalising your reactions to what is happening. Ultimately these reactions will express themselves, sometimes in unrelated and very negative ways. On the other hand, if you respond to situations and events in an unnecessarily negative way, then you will get a negative response. It is important to respond appropriately.

"If you always do what you have always done, you will always get the same result!"

Try this on for size and practice wearing it!

It is common to have difficulty expressing your own needs, while almost instantly recognising the needs of others

Learn to express your feelings in an assertive way.

Ask yourself:

- Do you make it clear what your needs are?
- Do you recognise your own needs?
- Do you know how to have your needs met - that is, without hurting others?
- Do you believe that it's not really machismo to blurt out your true emotions.
- Do you try to be lady-like and keep it all inside and whatever you do, don't let it show.
- Do you believe that no-one wants to hear much about what you have to say.
- Do you find it difficult to express yourself

So what type of things can make you get angry?

A reckless driver, your wallet's stolen, you locked your keys in the car, your wife went off with your best friend, (gee you miss him...), your only night in and your cable has gone on the blink, you go to the ATM, and it's empty,

List what triggers you to get angry
(besides being asked to make lists..):

....
....
....
....
....
....
....
....
....
....

How do you respond?
Yell and scream, put your fist through the wall, get moody,
grind your teeth, drive dangerously, terrorise your family and
friends, break valuable things, go silent or say "fine", storm out
of a room, leave for days or even hurt people physically. Then
there are the passive aggressive times when you are seething
inside but refuse to let it show. However you will not be able to
stop yourself from divulging the odd sarcastic remark or cynical overture. This is a typical attitude to those of you who have
difficulty in expressing how you really feel.

....
....
....
....
....

It's probably time that you learnt how to express yourself in a
more self-empowering way.

Getting sense and making change, starts here.

The three main approaches used for expressing angry feelings
are expression, suppression, and silence.

If you feel that you have anger management problems, consider help from a qualified and experienced therapist. You can un-learn self-effacing habits, and learn healthier ways in which to express yourself. Remember you have the ability, within you, to control your anger

Did you know that you can lower your heart rate, and blood pressure, by calming yourself down, and allowing your tumul-tuous feelings to subside?

Some hints for you:

- Learn to relax and count to 10
- Practice saying how you feel out loud and in private. You can even express how you feel in front of the mirror.

You can even express what you want in front of a mirror...

- When you are assertive you want to be in a calm state, be clear about what you are trying to say.
- Always be respectful to others.
- Drop the sarcastic and hostile behaviour – people absolutely hate that and it is a total social turn - off.
- Do not to intimidate those who may well be afraid of you, especially due to your previous outbursts.
- Stay in the moment and remain civilised.

- Say how you feel by beginning with "I felt hurt by what you said" or "I felt annoyed by what you did" When you have said how you feel, it is done, over, capiche! You do not need to over explain your thoughts and feelings. That will happen later on if it is necessary. Take small steps.
- Keep a journal and write down your triumphs no matter how small they are. They will quickly add up.
- Take up an activity that allows you to release pent up feelings of anger and anxiety. Kick boxing, martial arts or running.
- Do not take it out on others – they can't fix you but you will possibly lose them forever by insisting they do. Your wife, your mother, your brother or children are trying to cope with their own emotions too. Don't add to their problems.
- Discover the triggers for your anger e.g. jealousy, rejection, impatience etc
- Talk to people and try not to isolate yourself socially.
- Take up a self-esteem course.
- Engage in some voluntary work

Affirmation: "I acknowledge my feelings and always express them calmly".

How will your life improve once you make these changes:
Be specific and add detail:

Home-life:
....
....
....
....
....

Love-life:
....
....
....

....
....

Work-life:

....
....
....
....
....

Social-life:

....
....
....
....
....

"Man often becomes what he believes himself to be. If I keep on saying to myself that I cannot do a certain thing, it is possible that I may end by really becoming incapable of doing it. On the contrary, if I have the belief that I can do it, I shall surely acquire the capacity to do it even if I may not have it at the beginning."

Mahatma Ghandi

Depression

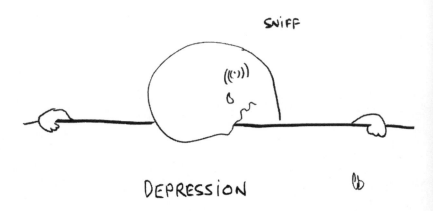

Depression is a state of mind and body. People sometimes think that depression is a bad thing and that it reflects "not being a strong enough man/woman, being weak, pathetic or emotionally out of control etc. It is often described as "looking down an endless dark tunnel without an inkling of light". Depression can leave you with feelings of desolation and pointlessness and a bleak picture of the future. Historically people have felt shameful about depression, as it was mainly associated with the stigma of mental illness and hysteria. Without a doubt, depression feels like a heavy weight and an overwhelming sense of despair.

Let's see what happens internally.

Biologically, neurons in your brain secrete and reabsorb neurological mediators, for example, serotonin and noradrenalin. In depression these mediators are reabsorbed too quickly.

Emotionally: You find it difficult to express yourself and accurately describe how you feel.

Physically: You feel listless and tired. Oftentimes people will complain about pains and aches. They may lose weight or put it on, find it hard to sleep at night and waken up too early.

Mentally: Mood swings become exaggerated leading to difficulty in concentration. Conversations tend to be melancholic with thoughts emphasising doom and gloom.

Depression, anxiety and elation are three corners of the one affective triangle. All three are normal reactions to life events. They only become a problem if the events they are a reaction to, do not get resolved.

Depression is analogous to physical pain. There are no nerve endings for pain. There are nerve endings for cold/heat, touch, vibration, position etc. If the stimulus on any of these nerve endings reaches a certain threshold, the sensation becomes painful. Pain is not there to make our lives miserable. It is there to warn us to avoid the stimulus – to take our hand off the kettle before we do harm to it. Depression is the emotional equivalent. Depression (and elation and anxiety) are there to tell us to sort out our emotional circumstances

Causes of depression:

Stress, Loss, Change and Conditioning

Current stress, past trauma, phobias, hormonal imbalance, sickness and poor nutrition.

Anything that is associated with loss and change can be a cause for depression. For example:

The loss of a parent, a sibling, a lover, your husband/wife, child and/or friend.

The sudden loss of a job, getting fired, being made redundant from your career or job, early or normal retirement.

Deteriorating health, loss of youth, loss of a limb, disease and / or impending mortality.

Change in living conditions, moving home, emigration, divorce or separation and trying to, or after having a baby.

Conditioning

Children learn social skills, communication skills and "fizzyology" from their family early in life. Growing up in a family, when one or both parents suffered with diagnosed, or undiagnosed depression, can leave a child acting similarly to their parents, without any other obvious cause for depression. Children have little discernment in judging what is appropriate, or inappropriate behaviour. They learn from what they see around them and act accordingly. *Monkey see, monkey do!*

Overwhelming demands on you in your life:

Being a busy mother/father, wife/husband, bread - winner, maintaining a size six, being super confident, keeping up appearances, persevering your youth, being a mentor, friend, partner, housekeeper, gardener and whore/stallion in the bedroom. This can result in stress leading to burn-out and ultimately depression.

Limited beliefs and perspective on life:

If you choose to believe that the earth is flat, you are right. If you choose to believe that you are fat, then you are right. If you choose to believe that you are unintelligent, then you are right. If you choose to believe that you are doomed to a life of misery and aloneness, well guess what? "That's right – you are right"

People will eventually get tired of trying to convince you that you are wrong. In fact they soon give up the challenge and come around to your way of thinking about you. The other good news is that they will leave you all to yourself to bask in your limiting belief system, in case it is contagious and they are not adequately inoculated against it. If you have poor expectations of yourself and the people in the world around you, then you will attract more of that. Remember that you will always get more of what you focus on in your life. As people, we respond to biofeedback. What are you telling yourself about your appearance, your dress sense, your body image, your ability to pull a chick, earn your living, and to have a happy and fulfilling life? Are you inundated with worries about your health, physique and/or finances? Well if you are, this can cause stress that leads to depression.

Signs and symptoms of depression are:

Decreased will or care in appearance,

Declining personal hygiene and shrinking interest in leisure and social activities.

Negative thinking, apathy and overwhelming periods of despondency and gloom.

Diminished desire for sex, affection and "joie de vivre".

Depression can result in a positive experience once it is professionally treated and dealt with in a productive way. Please keep in mind that people "do" depression. It is important for you not to think in terms of "being depressed". Depression is not an illness; it is a state, a sense, a feeling or mood. There are very specific ways in which depression is acted out. A person who is experiencing depression will hold their posture, head and facial expressions in particular ways. A person, who has a positive outlook in life generally sits with an upright and open posture, walks briskly with purpose, and tends to smile easily.

By taking the latest generic/brand-name medications or alternative potions/lotions, and complaining endlessly to your doctor, psychiatrist, counsellor or friends, you could get better, but the way to longer lasting health is by going to the next level. The first step is admitting that you have a problem. The next step is to take action, and learn skills to help you live with a positive outlook on life.

"The point to remember is that when you blame any outside force for any of your experience of life, you are literally giving away all your power and thus creating pain, paralysis and depression".

Susan Jeffers
("Feel the fear and do it anyway" Thinkarete.com)

Fear

FEAR

The two natural fears that we are born with are loud noises and falling. When faced with a threat, the body goes into an immediate state of apprehension and fear. Biologically, adrenaline, noradrenalin and cortisol are released into the blood stream, the heart quickens and blood vessels tighten. Your hands can become sweaty, face gets flushed, and mouth will dry.

This is commonly regarded as the fight, fright or flight response. Once the danger is subsided your body returns to normal homeostasis.

This fear response normally takes a couple of seconds and then subsides. In today's western world this stress response happens more frequently and lasts longer, leaving people in a prolonged fight, fright or flight state. Rather than alleviating the feeling we drink more coffee, smoke more cigarettes and guzzle more beers etc, adding more stress to the body. Try some relaxation techniques instead, like deeply breathing three times through the nose and exhaling each time through the mouth. Whilst doing this affirm "I am relaxed, at ease and in control of my life always" Repeat three times.

Fear is one of the most common emotional forces that motivate a person to take any type of action. What makes you run from a burning building, put petrol in your car, avoid parking on double yellow lines, swimming in shark invested waters, keep the metre running, being on time for work, apologise when you have done wrong? It is always due to being afraid of the possible negative outcomes that can occur.

The strongest emotional triggers we have are the fear of being betrayed and/or humiliated. Celebrities experience an overwhelming fear of being exposed as living like normal people. Whatever happens, we must not see celebrities doing ordinary things like mere mortals do. Whenever you are fearful of being found out in a lie or an event that you are shameful about, you

will do almost anything, and say anything to protect yourself -
even lie again!

What are you most fearful of?

....

....

....

....

....

*What is the worst thing that could happen to you as a result of
this?*

....

....

....

....

....

*What is the best thing that can happen to you as a result of
this?*
E.g. character building, letting go, and positive change of any kind

....

....

....

....

....

"*Inaction breeds doubt and fear. Action breeds confidence and courage. If you want to conquer fear, do not
sit home and think about it. Go out and get busy*".

Dale Carnegie

Guilt

According to Darwinian evolutionary theory, anything that survives generations of *natural selection* has to improve that organism's chance of survival. Otherwise, it would not be inherited by subsequent generations. Even a commonly held "negative" emotion such as guilt, must have some positive aspect, for it to have been naturally selected over those generations.

Guilt is a very powerful emotion. Guilt happens when you act against your own moral code. It is often what prevents you from doing something that you know is wrong, even when you know you can get away with it. It is also what will compel an individual to accept responsibility for an action that they have already got away with (e.g. the narrator in Edgar Allen Poe's "The Tell Tale Heart"). When the outcome of a guilt process is not positive, however, then guilt can be a very negative emotion. Guilt has been used by the powerful, for generations, to control the individual.

Religious guilt has also been used to control populations going back as far as the Genesis tale of Adam and Eve who were

scorned with original sin. All subsequent Christians are meant
to be born with this sin too. What makes matters worse is that
without the act of contrition to help make it all magically dis-
appear, you are doomed. Oh! We almost forgot that Eve was
the carrier of this emotional virus, enhancing the power of one
gender over the other..

Just think of the ludicrous notion that people are born into the
world with a predisposition to feeling bad about themselves.
It's similar to a hex or a scorn. Unresolved guilt is another way
of saying "I don't deserve another chance", "I am a bad and
irreparable person". The way emotions operate in the senso-
rial system is that emotions enjoy critical mass (or wild parties);
they grow and procreate. In other words they thrive on more
of what they have, not less. So the moral of the story is, if you
don't want it, change it or dump it (the guilt, we mean).

Unresolved guilt offers no positive resolution for you or anyone
else in the world. Have a dose of healthy regret instead. Ok so
"you blew it". Say "I am sorry" to the party concerned. It helps
to be sincere, forgive yourself and move on. Learn from your
mistake, your inappropriate judgement; back stabbing remark
and/or a bit of immaturity or stupidity. How bad could it be
anyway? So you stole your best friends high definition wide-
screen TV, Gucci bag, his girl friend or wife. Grab your "get out
of jail card" while it's available, pay the fine or do the time.

Feeling guilty wont make it all go away and it certainly will
not change your personal history, but being productive about
this predicament will pay dividends to your character and self
respect. Go on, and redeem yourself. Let the past go because
clearly, it is over and if you refuse to do this for yourself, then
you will keep reliving the event or worse still the feeling of guilt
over and over again. You create your feelings – the event is well
and truly over.

By not forcing yourself to feel bad, you might actually begin to feel relieved and happy again. Remember that guilt looks for punishment and/or forgiveness, so it is a cyclic pattern and becomes a self-fulfilling prophecy.

What triggers you to feel guilty anyway?

Worst case scenario:
Example:
Not returning emails and phone calls: This causes you to feel bad and guilty that you haven't lived up to your moral obligation and personal character. Then you feel that you have let people down and caused them upset or discomfort. Feeling even more discomfited and embarrassed you avoid the situation altogether. Time lapses and you never get the job done at all. You meet these people later on in life, and you try to avoid them - the guilt lives on.

You feel bad and will probably take similar inappropriate action with other aspects in your life. The guilt thrives like a fungus and your character wanes.

Your worst case scenario:
....
....
....
....
....

Best case scenario:
Example:
Forgetting to return emails and phone calls: You take the appropriate action, and deal with it by apology (not excuse). Your moral code and character is intact and you are completely guilt free. Remember, your self-esteem and reputation is based on how well you live up to your moral code and character.
Your best case scenario:

....
....
....
....
....

When and how do you forgive yourself and move on?
Do you give yourself forty lashes, drown your sorrows in vodka
and tonic, eat all around you or smoke yourself to death?
....
....
....
....
....

How long does your process last?
A week, a month, a year or a lifetime?
....
....
....
....
....

Who else suffers because of your guilt?
Your last best friend, your hairdresser, bartender, priest or rabbi?
....
....
....
....
....

"Be true to yourself"

Hate

This is a feeling of intense disdain. Hatred can be recognised in various cultures where discrimination and/or violence towards others is evident. Oftentimes people can thrive on these intense and negative feelings toward others. Racism and prejudice are the vital ingredients that embody hatred. Ask yourself, what are the benefits to having feelings of hate?

We can't think of one benefit to your health and well being, or to others that may be associated with hatred. Hatred is, however, the end result of other common emotions, such as ingrained fear, which do have positive survival attributes. Combine these with severe low self-esteem, and you unfortunately have a powerful negative force.

When you hold onto feelings of hatred towards others, you are bound to feel a combination of many negative emotions; bitterness, resentment, anger, and paranoia. Some people are prone to living a delusional life of despair; wanting connection but never experiencing it in a normal and natural way. The negative energy produced in such a situation, often gets released as anger towards those considered more fortunate. If you carry the burden of absolute hatred, get help to work through this. Otherwise you will end up a very sad and bitter person with many other unresolved issues in your life. When you hate, you are the person who suffers.

Ask yourself: who or what in your life benefits from hate?

Government Health Warning: "Hatred can seriously damage your health"

> *"Hate is too great a burden to bear. It injures the hater more than it injures the hated."*
>
> Coretta Scott King

Thinking too much

When you think too much you go over and over negative thoughts in your head. It's like a game of *'snakes and ladders'* - down the snakes and up the ladders! Women, due to their genetic and hormonal disposition are notorious for analysing, cross-examining, judging and condemning in less than ten point six seconds. There are various types of overthinking which men are also prone to. Although most men are highly skilled decision makers, many become immersed in overthinking about issues such as; getting married, buying a house, relocating and changing careers. During times of self-evaluation, over thinking can be obsessive and cause depression. Questions like: *"who am I?"*, *"why am I here?"*, *"what is my purpose in life?"*, *"does anyone really care about me?"* *"How does the flush in the toilet work?"* etc., run around our brains. Overthinking is tough on the mind and although you are seeking answers, these are questions with no easy solutions. In the meantime you create anxiety, endless doubt and eventual ill health.

One of the negative aspects of overthinking is that it is bad for your health. It invariably brings on negative emotions, such as anxiety, confusion, stress, depression, hopelessness and loss of control. These can build up like an emotional pressure cooker, and may even lead to mental illness.

On the positive side, overthinking may alert you to a problem that you need to deal with logically. Overthinking may alert you to a disempowering pattern of thinking and the emotional rollercoaster that you get caught up in, on a regular basis

Task:

What do you find yourself overthinking about?

Getting old, your weight, your health, your family, keeping your wife/husband interested, an affair, money, being fulfilled in life etc

....
....
....
....
....

Do you ever reach a solution?

Yes [ ], No [ ]

Suggested steps that you may take are:

Stop the 'pinking thinking'. Be firm with yourself. Think it through and take appropriate action.

Reframe the situation by seeing it from a more positive perspective.

Write your thoughts down on paper. This compartmentalises, releases the anxiety and creates some clarity for you.

Make a decision, any decision, and stick with that decision for twenty-four hours. Do not waver until the twenty–four hours time slot is up. Then you can change your mind if you must.

Get out of your head and into your body. Move your body and/or your vocal cords! Go for a run or swim, dance in the kitchen, play an instrument or sing out loud.

Pamper yourself; go for a sauna, have a massage, watch a DVD and/or have a face and body treatment.

Remember to visualise your outcome in the positive for five to ten minutes each day. Practice your strategies and be assured that overthinking can eventually be a thing of the past. Always give yourself feedback when you successfully interrupt the overthinking patterns.   Keep a note of your triumphs starting today.

Today I interrupted overthinking by:
....
....
....
....
....

Tomorrow I intend to resolve overthinking by:
....
....
....
....
....

My reward to myself for this is:
....
....
....
....
....

"If you change the way you look at things, the things you look at change."

Dr Wayne Dyer

MUSIC

EVERYONE IS OUT OF TUNE EXCEPT OUR JOHNNY...

"Music is the universal language of mankind".
Henry Wadsworth Longfellow, ("Outre-Mer")

"If I were not a physicist, I would probably be a musician. I often think in music. I live my daydreams in music. I see my life in terms of music".

Albert Einstein

EINSTEIN

Since the beginning of time, music has been a fundamental part of our existence.

Music is food for the soul – a panacea for the mind. Music connects peoples throughout the world. When people can't say it they sing it. Love-songs and melancholy tunes travel deep into the hearts and spirits of everyone. Music is clearly a universal language. Regardless of race, colour and gender, music remains steadfast through out time, while changing with each generation. Music has a deep and permanent impact on the body, mind and spirit.

music is clearly A UNIVERSAl lANGUAGE

In the more contemporary and advanced hospitals worldwide, music is becoming an integral component in health care today. Music is used as part of both pre and post operative treatments. It is also used for expectant and nursing mothers. This helps to de-stress and relax, and accelerate the healing process.

"It is more important to know what sort of person has a disease than to know what sort of disease a person has."
Hippocrates (460-377 B.C.)

A HiPPO CRATE

The Alternative/Complementary therapy genre incorporates music as a vital means to health and well being. Alternative therapies include music therapy, meditation, exercise and dance therapy, relaxation and massage to name but a few. Music, in addition to, and as part of, most therapies creates a more profound effect on the overall experience. Music therapy in effect can bring about positive psychological, emotional, and physical changes in a person. The benefits include relaxation, focus, recuperation and general healing of the mind, body and spirit.

"Why waste money on psychotherapy when you can listen to the B Minor Mass?"

Michael Torke

Music as a healing influence, can positively affect health and behaviour in all age groups and genders. The healing properties that come from music therapy have been around for centuries. In fact during wars in times past, musicians visited soldiers in hospitals where the badly wounded, sufferers of shell shock and other post traumatic stress disorders were greatly aided and felt relief through melody. Along with patients, doctors and nurses alike noted the positive physical and emotional results and also the relaxing effect on the staff and in the hospital atmosphere, which was duly appreciated.

The vast benefits that music therapy can provide in emotional and physical health and well being are well known, there are more avenues in which music can enrich and help heal. When an individual decides to pursue their own interest in music the benefits can far exceed expectation. Some avenues that may be of interest to you are:

Discovering music.

Learning how to play an instrument or two.

Understanding staff music; a language all onto its own.

Writing music; to one or more instruments.

Writing song through lyrics; writing your thoughts and feelings to music.

Discovering your voice and that of others; voice training.

Teaching music and song.

Being open to all types of sounds and vibrations.

THE DISCOVERY OF MUSIC

As well as playing music, research reveals that writing music is a most therapeutic and catalytic form of releasing emotional pain.

Music is emotional and it can stir up all kinds of feelings within each one of us, so discussion of music is also very powerful. Discussing music gives you a voice to articulate your feelings, views and interpretations about all types of musicians and music. It also helps to inspire patience and healthy debate. Music imagery and music performance including musical comedy and opera productions are relaxing, moving and educational.

For many years, nature sounds such as birds singing, waves breaking against the shore, waterfalls, and the wind have been some of the most soothing and relaxing sounds for everyone including clients and patients alike during specific treatments or while simply relaxing and taking some 'time out'.

Music is utilised in helping a person to strengthen their respiratory system, throat, and facial muscles through singing. Music through creative dance and physical exercise, encompassing similar movements to yoga or Tai Chi helps build and strengthen the physical body by improving co-ordination skills especially after a road traffic accident, arthritis or stroke etc.

This can also support a person to re-establish better co-ordination and ease in movement which is vital in the prevention of minor accidents (trips and falls) and the maintenance of better posture and structural balance.

"Music's the medicine of the mind".

John A. Logan

MUSIC is THE MEDICINE
OF THE MIND

Situations where music can play a significant role:

cancer patients, children with ADHD, and others.

pain management, depression,

mobilisation, relaxation, muscle tension relief

lowering blood pressure (which can also reduce the risk of stroke and other health problems over time), boost immunity,

Examples:

Heart Patients derived the same benefits from listening to 30 minutes of classical music as they did from taking 10 mg of the anti-anxiety medication diazepam at a Baltimore hospital.

Migraine sufferers were trained to use music, imagery and relaxation techniques to reduce the frequency, intensity and duration of their headaches...in a California State University study.

People who listened to light classical music for 90 minutes while editing a manuscript increased accuracy by 21%...in a University of Washington study.

Students who listened to 10 minutes of Mozart prior to taking SATs had higher scores than students who weren't exposed to music...at the University of California.

Ida Goldman (90 year-old testifying at senate hearings; August 1, 1991): "Before I had surgery they told me I could never walk again. But when I sat and listened to music, I forgot all about the pain," said Goldman, who walked with assistance during the hearing.

Dr. Oliver Sacks ("Awakenings," "The Man Who Mistook His Wife for a Hat") reports that patients with neurological disorders who cannot talk or move are often able to sing, and sometimes even dance, to music. Its advocates say music therapy also can help ease the trauma of grieving, lessen depression and provide an outlet for people who are otherwise withdrawn.

Music for relaxation
- as a past time for everyday use
For your own private and personal enjoyment, writing or playing music is a wonderful hobby with many positive side affects. First of all it constantly challenges you to improve and there is really no end to that. Also the more you practice, the more you improve and hopefully gain a sense of satisfaction with your ac-

complishments, regardless of how small they may seem. Playing your own music is conducive to healing as it helps to completely switch off the outside world and retreat into your own internal world of peace and at times tolerable frustration. It helps alleviate stress and improve creativity and self-confidence. Music also enhances social relationships as you can join groups, clubs and bands. When playing with others you may learn new techniques and styles as well as improve through other people's expertise. Socially, your talent to play music can also help to create a light and happy atmosphere anywhere you go. The ladies love a guy who plays music so it can help improve your pulling power and/or love life.

On the other hand playing or listening to music too loudly and/or over a long period of time can cause hearing damage. This can be worsened especially if music is listened to from an early age and over a long period of time.

Strong and deliberate beats invigorate brain wave activity, which are in sync with the beat. Quickened beats bring sharper concentration and more alert thinking, and slower rhythms induce a sense of calm. The fluctuation and change in brainwave activity levels stimulated by music enable the brain to alternate speeds more easily on its own. In other words the effects of music has a lasting impression on your state of mind and general well being because its effects last, long after the music has stopped. Music lives on in our hearts and minds long after it is over.

As the brain waves fluctuate with music there are significant physiological reactions in the body as brain waves fluctuate as a result of changing rhythm's and beats. Many of these alterations include the change in breathing and muscle tension. Heart rate either slows down or quickens up. The autonomic nervous system is stimulated and relaxation or excitement will result. The vibrations of music and other sounds are sensed and absorbed into the skin and bones. Relaxation improves the healing. Restoration in the body is achieved, while stimulating music can also help alleviate the symptoms and effects of depression, sharpening mental capacity and alertness.

"Just as certain selections of music will nourish your physical body and your emotional layer, so other musical works will bring greater health to your mind".

Hal A. Lingerman

Music probably began from the rhythm of the heartbeat, and the vibration of the bow. Every country around the globe has its own unique sound and vibration. From the Masai and Zulu tribes to the Samurai and American Indian tribes, music has its own individual resonance and depth. Music portrays feelings and emotions that were prevalent in regions and countries in times past, testifying to its people's cares and woes, sentiments, losses and joy's. Traditional music, with it's tempo and lyrics, signified the voids and needs that each country had; rights or values that they were striving to obtain; equally in celebration of their triumphs and victories. The tribal spirit with its ancient rhythms has the power to illuminate and awaken vibrancy, vitality, inspiration and courage within the souls of many, through their instruments and vocals alike

The structure and many rhythms, melodies and high frequencies of Mozart's music stimulate and charge the creative and motivational regions of the brain. However, you don't have to listen only to Mozart-or even classical music. Everything from Gregorian chant to New Age, jazz, big band, Latin, dance and rock compositions can produce different benefits.

Harmony helps you to release painful or angry feelings or boost happy feelings.

To stimulate the body, play your favourite dance music - hip hop music, salsa, disco, jigs and reels (1980's music comes to mind).

List some of you favourite dance styles:

....
....
....
....
....

Describe how it makes you feel:

....
....
....
....
....

> *"I think music in itself is healing. It's an explosive expression of humanity. It's something we are all touched by. No matter what culture we're from, everyone loves music".*
>
> Billy Joel

Task:
Some of the reasons you might want to tap into your unconscious mind are to become more creative, mentally stimulated and motivated.
In order to tap into your unconscious mind try moving your body now.
By listening to upbeat music you can envigorate your right brain hemisphere which is your creative and imaginative side. Do it for approximiately three minutes.

Music examples include: Mozart, Beethovan, Handel and Brahms

....
....
....
....
....

Afterward write down how you feel mentally, emotionally and physically:

....

....

....

....

....

Task:
In order to relax and to relieve tension in your mind and body listen to the opposite style of music where the tempo is slow and easy.

Music examples include: Chopin, Nat King Cole, Bing Crosby

....

....

....

....

....

Afterwards, write down how you feel mentally, emotionally and physically:

....

....

....

....

....

"Music washes away from the soul the dust of everyday life".

Red Auerbach

Alzheimer's and other forms of dementia are some of the most heart breaking diseases to endure for patients, families and friends. Dementia is a worsening and fatal disease, which causes shrinking of the brain. Although when Alzheimer's begins to destroy brain cells there are no outward symptoms, many recognise this disease in sufferers by their decreasing loss of concentration and memory, and their increasing tendency to wandering. There are other cognitive deficits, which will eventually result in significant personality changes and total loss of control over bodily functions.

One of the earliest signs of dementia is difficulty in communication, even of the smallest kind. Eventually signs include notable difficulties in comprehending, discernment and rational thinking. As the disease worsens the individual's family, work and social life is adversely affected. Eventually it becomes impossible for the sufferer to manage by his or her own devices, and home care or hospitalisation will be necessary.

While some of us experience mild memory losses with ageing, people with Alzheimer's have a more noticeable and rapid decline in memory and other cognitive skills. With respect to memory they may forget where they leave things or to whom they are speaking. With the progression of Alzheimer's disease, disorientation, confusion, and anxiety follow, as well as behavioural disturbances, including seclusion, depression, agitation and anger. This is where music therapy can be used as an intervention to help soothe, calm and relax the person who is suffering. Music is also beneficial for the family members, whose stress and worry sometimes go un-noticed.

The application of music therapy for Alzheimer's patients is relatively new. However it is quickly becoming well known as a form of progressive therapy in the care of Alzheimer's and other dementia in hospitals and clinics around the world.

MUSIC AND DEMENTIA

As Music therapy has a positive effect on patients and people alike, a simple therapy that is known to help with cognitive and social skills is singing popular songs such as "doe, a deer" and encouraging them to sing in the blanks;

"Do, a deer, a female....
Re a drop of golden..
Me, a name I call....
Fa a long, long way to..
So, a needle pulling..."

This type of singing is excellent, as the patient learns to recall the next word in the song. This is done in a group and family can participate also. Music can help relax patients when they feel distressed and anxious. Also it is noted that by listening to old familiar music from their youth, the elderly feel their moods lift and this helps make them feel better in general.

By frequenting local musical events and gatherings, the elderly get to meet up with people and friends in the community. Recreation of this kind is invaluable for all ages, especially the elderly who sometimes feel that they are 'passed it' and 'left out to pasture' by their family. Listening to and playing musical instruments or singing along with a group is an excellent way to feel connected; more youthful and alive. Movement through music is also highly beneficial for the elderly, and can help with degenerative diseases like arthritis and osteoporosis and stiff muscles and joints. Movement is excellent to help improve circulation and flexibility.

Everyone loves one form of music or another, indeed many of us are devoted to our favourite singers, bands and musicians. Music can either motivate us or relax us. Many experts now believe and embrace the notion that music can promote the individuals psychological and physical healing process, which includes children and the elderly

Task:
With an elderly grand parent, father, mother, aunt or uncle or friend; take them out on a musical evening that you know they will enjoy. Present them with a dance card and ensure that you give them a dance or two.

Plan the date:
....

Venue:
....

How did it go?
....

Music is incredibly important for the emotional and mental development in children. It helps them to learn easily and enhances their memory skills. Notice how children can musically recite nursery rhymes, alphabets, spellings and times-tables.

Research shows that children from a very young age respond positively to music. A baby in the wombcan hear sounds from 20 weeks after conception.

From the moment a baby is conceived, music can have a calming effect on the expectant mother, which obviously will have an even greater effect on the baby in her womb. A relaxed and happy mother is a relaxed and happy baby.

In the formative years of a child's life they learn to hear sounds. They quickly recognise the sound of their mother's cooing voice and the effect this has on them is noticeable, as they might smile and wiggle their little legs and arms which would imply comfort, safety and security. Later they learn to distinguish comforting tones from threatening ones.

Children learn from observing what is going on around them, rather than from what they are told to do. There is little point in telling a baby what to do, because babies don't understand. In any case 'what children see, children do' so they attempt to copy what they see around them. Humans never again learn so much, so fast, as they do when they are children. Imitation is a profound learning tool for them. By *singing* nursery rhymes, spellings and times-tables, a child learns easily and effortlessly. Moreover, when mom, dad and family members participate in the *sing–alongs* a child learns to learn in a secure and fun environment, therefore associating learning as fun, secure and unthreatening. This is a great way to begin a successful life.

Children should be encouraged to be their own musician. First of all by shaking their rattles, drumming their drums and listening to "twinkle dee - twinkle dum" sounds. Next they should be urged and persuaded to start hammering away at pot and pans etc. It is good for a child to discover the varying sounds they can actually create all on their own; from hollow beats to sharp beat and high pitched tones. Some known toy instruments that improve a child's mental and emotional development are drums, keyboards, and xylophones.

The "Mozart Effect" is meant to enhance a child's learning capacity and yet scientists have discredited this notion. The

"Mozart "Effect" may have gained popularity over the years due to various research programmes that reveal that by listening to classical musical children become more intelligent. The effects from listening to, learning and participating in music is astounding. For example children's memory is improved and their ability to think logically enhanced. This, in turn provides a good foundation in learning mathematics and science subjects later to come.

Learning music and dancing to music enhances hand-eye co-ordination that leads to better motor skills. Concentration and the ability to focus, is refined through the practice of reading music and practising tunes. This helps to improve the ability to learn all other subjects in school. Playing music in-groups, bands and choirs helps create team spirit, which enhances social development and self - confidence

Music is incredibly important to a child's development on many levels. When children take up the demanding roles of adults in this fast paced society, at least they will have learnt one of the easiest and most rewarding ways to unwind and relax; with music

Music Therapy is not widely offered by general practitioners, but is available on the NHS in Wales, U.K., to patients with physical and psychological problems. Such therapy was introduced shortly after the Second World War when it became evident how music could soothe shell-shocked war heroes when other therapies failed.

Oliver Sacks, MD, FRCP, of "Awakenings" fame, catapulted music therapy to the next level in the 1960s when he made some remarkable discoveries at the Beth Abraham Hospital in New York.

"I first saw the immense therapeutic powers of music in 80 individuals who were victims of encephalitis lethargica, a viral sleeping sickness," Sacks says. "Most of them had been 'frozen', absolutely motionless, for decades. Rosalie B, a patient who had a severe form of parkinsonism tended to remain transfixed for hours a day, completely motionless.

"We had only to say Opus 49, however, to see her whole body, posture and expression change."

Sacks also notes it is important to use music that suits the individual. "Another patient," he explains, "has not been able to retain any new memories since the 1970s, but if we talk about or play his favorite Grateful Dead songs, his amnesia is bypassed."

Scholars believe the reason humans respond so well to music is because there is something intrinsically musical about the brain's structure.

Policymakers and health authorities had, until recently however, considered past findings merely anecdotal but a recent study at the Chelsea and Westminster Hospital, has challenged this.

The study, spearheaded by Rosalia Staricoff, PhD, was the first of its kind to actively look for scientific proof that directly links music with health.

The research took place over a six-month period in various wards or units where live performances of light, classical and world music was played to patients.

"We found the levels of blood pressure can be reduced in pregnant women waiting for their appointments in the high-risk ante-natal clinic," Staricoff explains. "We also researched into the amount of drugs needed to induce sleep prior to anaesthesia. Patients exposed to cheerful music during pre-operative preparations needed significantly less."

This has all come at a time when the British Medical Journal has suggested the government spend more money on the arts and less on medicine. A recent report states around 50 billion is currently invested in healthcare each year and 300 million on the arts. Their suggestion is to divert 0.5 percent of healthcare budget into the arts to improve the health of our country.

One-to-one music therapy sessions can take many different forms and can involve anything from chanting or drumming to using synthesizers as a patient interacts with their sonic environment.

GIM therapy (Guided Imagery and Music), alternatively, involves a number of art mediums and approaches, which can have a very penetrative effect on the subconscious. In such a session a patient is relaxed into a meditative state and various pieces of music are played that help trigger mental images which unlock unresolved life issues.

"I do not think that there is anything that can be 'treated' with music," Staricoff emphasizes, "but it is important to recognize that music can play a vital role in healthcare. It will be a great day when all medical staff consider and recognize this and then implement the recommendations for its use."

Quotes:

"Without music, life is a journey through a desert."

Pat Conroy

"Music is the vernacular of the human soul."

Geoffrey Latham

"Music is a beautiful opiate, if you don't take it too seriously."

Theodore Mungers

"I would advise you to keep your overhead down; avoid a major drug habit; play everyday, and take it in front of other people. They need to hear it, and you need them to hear it".

James Taylor

"The gods who have been appointed to be our companions in the dance, have given us the pleasurable sense of harmony and rhythm; and so they stir us to life, and we follow them, joining together in dances and songs".

Plato

"Bands that play the blues are usually not very good. The blues are a personal thing, and should usually be played by some guy who is very ugly and is half full of whiskey. Without this how can you have the blues...can good-looking people get the blues? They can, but they have to be on heroin."

Author Unknown
– circulating on the internet.

"Music is either good or bad, and it's got to be learned. You got to have balance."

Louis Armstrong

"Music is well said to be the speech of angels."
Thomas Carlyle

"All music is important if it comes from the heart."
Carlos Santana

"Most of us go to our grave with our music still inside of us."
Unknown

"A painter paints pictures on canvas. But musicians paint their pictures on silence."
Leopold Stokowski

"Without music life would be a mistake."
Friedrich Wilhelm Nietzsche

"Take a music bath once or twice a week for a few seasons. You will find it is to the soul what a water bath is to the body."
Oliver Wendell Holmes

"And the night shall be filled with music,
And the cares that infest the day
Shall fold their tents like the Arabs
And as silently steal away."
Henry Wadsworth Longfellow,
("The Day Is Done"*)*

"The doctor of the future will give no medicine, but will interest his patients in the care of the human frame, in diet, and in the cause and prevention of disease."
Thomas Edison, Inventor

"He who sings scares away his woes."
Cervantes

"Music was my refuge. I could crawl into the space between the notes and curl my back to loneliness."

Maya Angelou,
(Gather Together in My Name)

"Music is what feelings sound like."

Author Unknown

"There's music in the sighing of a reed;
There's music in the gushing of a rill;
There's music in all things, if men had ears;
Their earth is but an echo of the spheres."

Lord Byron

"Music is the mediator between the spiritual and the sen-
sual life."

Ludwig van Beethoven

"I have my own particular sorrows, loves, delights; and
you have yours. But sorrow, gladness, yearning, hope,
love, belong to all of us, in all times and in all places.
Music is the only means whereby we feel these emotions
in their universality."

H.A. Overstreet

"My idea is that there is music in the air, music all around
us; the world is full of it, and you simply take as much as
you require."

Edward Elgar

"Alas for those that never sing.
But die with all their music in them!"

Oliver Wendell Holmes

"Music is your own experience, your thoughts, your wisdom. If you don't live it, it won't come out of your horn."

Charlie Parker

"Life can't be all bad when for ten dollars you can buy all the Beethoven sonatas and listen to them for ten years."

William F. Buckley, Jr.

"Music cleanses the understanding; inspires it, and lifts it into a realm which it would not reach if it were left to itself."

Henry Ward Beecher

"Music is the wine which inspires one to new generative processes, and I am Bacchus who presses out this glorious wine for mankind and makes them spiritually drunken."

Ludwig Van Beethoven

"Music is the wine that fills the cup of silence."

Robert Fripp

"[An intellectual] is someone who can listen to the "William Tell Overture" without thinking of the Lone Ranger."

John Chesson

"Were it not for music, we might in these days say, the Beautiful is dead."

Benjamin Disraeli

"Music is what feelings sound like."

Author Unknown

"There's music in the sighing of a reed;
There's music in the gushing of a rill;
There's music in all things, if men had ears:
Their earth is but an echo of the spheres."

Lord Byron

"Musical compositions, it should be remembered, do not inhabit certain countries, certain museums, like paintings and statues. The Mozart Quintet is not shut up in Salzburg: I have it in my pocket."

Henri Rabaud

"Music is the poetry of the air."

Richter

"If I were to begin life again, I would devote it to music. It is the only cheap and unpunished rapture upon earth."

Sydney Smith

"He who hears music, feels his solitude peopled at once."

Robert Browning

"The Irish gave the bagpipes to the Scots as a joke, but the Scots haven't got the joke yet."

Oliver Herford

"Music expresses that which cannot be said and on which it is impossible to be silent."

Victor Hugo

"...where music dwells lingering - and wandering on as loth to die..."

William Wordsworth,
"Within King's College Chapel, Cambridge"

GRATITUDE
THANKS A LOT!

"The word gratitude, appreciation, or thankfulness is a positive emotion or attitude in acknowledgement of a benefit that one has received or will receive".

Wikipedia

"He is a wise man who does not grieve for the things which he has not, but rejoices for those which he has."

Epictetus

This chapter is about acknowledging and being truly grateful for what you already have in your life in every conceivable way. From the air that you breathe to the home in which you live. This chapter is about being appreciative for all that you think you haven't got but actually do.

We would like to take you on a journey as though you are in a majestic mansion and from each window you gaze, there is a completely different landscape. Every time you look through a window you observe the world in an altered and distinctly different way. You will observe yourself in it from a changed perspective as well. As we move on through this chapter, you will soon notice how these windows will further become your windows of opportunity!

Why a mansion? You might ask. In your dreams, which are the doorway to your subconscious mind; mansions usually symbolise the effect, which the outside world has on you.

Subconsciously they reveal how the world is a strong influence in shaping our thoughts and feelings. Mansions can often link to situations where your feelings about yourself and about others are very much related and closely connected. They link you to situations and symbolically describe how your actions truly impact upon the lives of others. A mansion can also stand for, or typify your own personality, given the archetypal fluctuations of your make-up. A mansion is regarded as the home to your soul. Enjoy the journey of your transformation.

Visualise your mansion now:

Where is it:

....

....

....

....

....

What does it look like:

....
....
....
....
....

Where are you in your mansion:

....
....
....
....
....

Now it's time to look out through the window of uneven and bewildered landscape. Through this window you may witness desperation and cruelty.

WINDOW NO 1: Not On Your Doorstep

We live in a world of inequality. There are many that seem to have plenty and there are those others who live in extreme poverty and deprivation.

862 million people across the world are hungry.

Every day, almost 16,000 children die due to hunger-related reasons. It is estimated that one child dies every five seconds. One out of every eight children under the age of twelve in the United States goes to bed hungry every night. Statistics bring to our attention that every year approximately 15 million children die of absolute hunger and an estimated one individual dies from hunger every three seconds.

State of the World's Children 2008--Child Survival.
UNICEF. January 2008.

Infomercials, campaigners, charity organisations and well meaning citizens do their absolute best to bring to public attention, and that of our governments, the anguish in which people exist.

Such well-known public figures that come to mind are Irish notables such as Bob Geldof and Paul Hewson *AKA* 'Bono'. Bob Geldof, with the help of his friends and associates changed the consciousness of world hunger in the western world. Belligerently defying bureaucracy and stalemate constitution, Geldof was a crusader for the impoverished in Africa, who are rarely heard of or publicly known. Many others followed in his footsteps. These people are like saints amongst us who quietly fly under the media and government radar, but engender such a massive impetus to the betterment of our world. Governments continue to debate on economic fronts, the best way to solve the worldwide problem of hunger and inequality. Unfortunately, people keep dying in the process.

Craving for food is the most extreme form of poverty, where individuals or families cannot even afford to deliver on their most basic need for food.
Hunger manifests itself in many ways other than starvation and famine. Most poor people who battle with hunger deal with chronic malnutrition and vitamin and mineral deficiencies. This can result in deficient growth; infirmity and a greater likelihood of illness and disease. The lack of food intake can contribute to declining levels of mental and emotional growth. It can also hinder foetal development and shorten life expectancy.

According to the United Nations Food and Agriculture; one in twelve people worldwide is malnourished, including one hundred and sixty million children under the age of five.

There are numerous physical, emotional, and social effects that result from under - nourishment due to hunger and poverty. For example people's general health and well being immensely decline as their ability to work is lessened due to fragmented health and lack of employment. The individual's confidence in themselves, hope for their future and outlook on life is severed and disappears like the food they see in their minds eye. Their sense of fair play and justice in the world becomes a far away way dream or completely diminished.

Every year, more than 20 million low-birth weight babies are born in developing countries. These babies risk dying in infancy, while those who survive, often suffer lifelong physical and cognitive disabilities.
Low Birthweight: Country, Regional and Global Estimates.
World Health Organization. 2004.

The four most common childhood illnesses are diarrhoea, acute respiratory illness, malaria and measles. Each of these illnesses is both preventable and treatable. Yet, again, poverty interferes in parents' ability to access immunisations and medicines. Chronic malnutrition on top of insufficient treatment greatly increases a child's risk of death.
©2007 Bread for the World & Bread for the World Institute · 50 F Street, NW, Suite 500 · Washington, DC 20001 · USA Tel. 202-639-9400 · 800-82-BREAD · Fax 202-639-9401

WINDOW NO 2: The Past

Ireland
In 1846 – 1851, Ireland endured a famine where people died from hunger and related illness and disease. This was due to a diseased potato crop, caused by a fungus, Phytophthora infestans, commonly known as blight, which had spread from North America to Europe. The blight destroyed the potato harvest throughout Europe including Ireland. Statisticians estimate that 1,000,000 people lost their lives primarily due to the famine. An excess of one million Irish people left their country, never to return and emigrated to England, America and Australia and elsewhere. They sadly left their homeland

to find work, send money back to their impoverished families and to begin a new life abroad. Following this emigration millions continued to leave Ireland for decades that followed. It is said that the Irish population has never resumed to its formative population prior to the famine or The Great Hunger. As part of the Irish culture, including other events in it's history, the Irish people manifested a believe system that would stick with them for generations to come.

For years after this disaster the Irish people continued to carry and pass down the consciousness of 'lack', never 'having enough', 'always needing more' and believing that 'it will be taken from them in the end anyway.'

WINDOW NO 3: The Current and Existing Epidemic

The spread of HIV/AIDS epidemic is a major obstacle in the fight against hunger and poverty in developing countries.
In half of the countries in sub-Saharan Africa, per capita economic growth is estimated to be falling by between 0.5 and 1.2 percent each year as a direct result of AIDS
.
Infected adults also leave behind children and elderly relatives, who have little means to provide for themselves. In 2003, 12 million children were newly orphaned in southern Africa, a number expected to rise to 18 million in 2010. Since the epidemic began, 25 million people have died from AIDS, which has caused more than 15 million children to lose at least one parent. For its analysis, UNICEF uses a term that illustrates the gravity of the situation; child-headed households - minors orphaned by HIV/AIDS who are raising their siblings.
"The Global Challenge of HIV/AIDS." The Population Bulletin Vol. 61, No. 1. Population Reference Bureau. March 2006.
2006 AIDS Epidemic Update.
Joint United Nations Programme on AIDS. December 2006.
http://library.thinkquest.org/C002291/high/present/stats.htm

WINDOW NO 4: *The Potential Future*

It is incredibly sad to face the fact that so many people are suffering in the world every second of every minute. Indeed, we do not have to look that far away to notice people we pass and ignore on our streets; begging, sick or alone. There may be moments in your busy schedule when you don't even have the time to acknowledge people or give strangers a short glance with some eye contact.

Sometimes all it takes is a smile to make that permanent difference in someone's life that says, "I see you". There is no way of knowing what troubles or difficulties a person may have. They could be absorbed with some heart wrenching news about their own, or a family members health. There could be a loss, a deep sadness or severe depression that they are enduring. They could feel that no one in the world can see them or cares about their existence. Imagine a person on your street during a busy lunch hour whose eyes meet yours; wouldn't you want to make sure that they felt a little warmth from you that costs you nothing? It's just a simple smile or an acknowledgement. Give your smiles away as if you have nothing to lose but everything to gain.

> *"Everytime you smile at someone, it is an action of love, a gift to that person, a beautiful thing".*
>
> Mother Teresa

WINDOW NO 5: *Your Life Of Gratitude*

Now, take some time and consider the extraordinary abundance in your life:

Task:
What did you have for breakfast, lunch and dinner and the nibbly bits in between? The purpose of this exercise is not to make you feel guilty. Rather, it is just to point out how much you actually have.

....
....
....
....
....

"Thank God--every morning when you get up--that you have something to do which must be done, whether you like it or not. Being forced to work, and forced to do your best, will breed in you a hundred virtues which the idle never know."

Charles Kingsley

Task:
What have you thrown away lately or given to friends and family?
E.g.Clothes, food, toys, make up, CD's, DVD's, books, even money

....
....
....
....
....

See how kind hearted or generous you are! Regardless of your motives for giving; you *do* give, donate or contribute. You do this because you have it to give, and you have the heart to take action.

Have you ever noticed how easy it would be not to read the staggering statistics of the previous paragraphs; watch the news or read the headlines in the evening newspapers? You may not want your day to begin by or end with the frivolity of negativity that could affect your fragile energy or demeanour for the day. The truth is, is that you need to know, and to keep abreast of our changing times and crisis's that affect people all around the world and the health of our planet earth.

We must not turn a blind eye to such happenings. Although you might ask, "but what's the point in knowing all this what difference could I possibly make?"

Task:
Write down three tasks that you can do to help make a difference in the global / community hunger or deprivation?

....
....
....
....
....

In other words whatever, whatever you do in this moment can make a difference in the greater scheme of things.

When a butterfly flutters its wings on one side of the earth it can cause the weather to change thousands of miles away. Just a fragile little butterfly! "The butterfly effect", as it is known, states that the shift of air caused by a single butterfly is enough to change the weather patterns across the world. Life is a chain reaction.

The world is your oyster

We can acquire almost anything we want from a pushbike to an aeroplane, a kiss to a relationship, a penny to a pound and weekend holiday to a round trip world cruise. We can be so much and have so much in our lifetime.

In case you don't like the meal you order in a restaurant, you can always send it back to the kitchen, have it reheated, altered in some way or replaced. You can replace your mobile phone, laptop and car at the "drop of a hat" if you chose to. For instance, when in company that you find uninteresting or dull, you can make the best of it or you can leave. You can leave your partner, wife and husband if you want, or you can work on the relationship. The list goes on and on. Let's face it; we are spoilt for choice. Nevertheless, we convince ourselves that we are stuck in a rut, stressed, there's no way out and life is terrible, because I still don't have the fast car, house in the country, super bod, eternal youth, perfect home, super family and super friends.

Make a list of what you tell yourself will make your life perfect beginning each sentence with:

"If only I had...., or could be...., my life would be better, perfect etc". Include the reasons why:

If only I had:

....

....

....

....

....

My life would be better or more *perfect* because:

....

....

....

....

....

If only I could be:

....

....

....

....

....

My life would be better or more *perfect* because:

....

....

....

....

....

Now, think of some of the good things that already exist in your life. Write down what you have. When doing this exercise just write down whatever comes to mind.

My life is wonderful because:

....
....
....
....
....

Other people's lives are better because of me. List some of the reasons why:

....
....
....
....
....

I like you sooo much, I think you're terrific!

Often it is easy to take people for granted. Family, friends and lovers are so comfortable to be with, that they can feel like a favourite old chair. Not that you might want to sit on them all day, but that you feel so relaxed being with them. It is so easy to get absorbed in how you feel, with no drama, with life going pretty well. "What more could you want or need?" you might ask. We might answer that you could be more appreciative of the people you are closely connected to. If you find it hard to tell them how you feel, give them a note that says thank you for being you, or a flower that represents beauty and life, or a pillow that symbolises a soft place to rest your head and dream sweet dreams.

There are many ways in which you can show appreciation for another. Let go of the need to get a reaction or a response. As soon as you give or express appreciation in anyway, that feeling becomes their feeling, let go and move away.

> *"Let us be grateful to people who make us happy; they are the charming gardeners who make our souls blossom."*
> Marcel Proust

Who in your life do you appreciate?

....
....
....
....
....

How do you express appreciation to each person?

....
....
....
....
....

How do you intend to express appreciation for them?

....
....
....
....
....

"The deepest craving of human nature is the need to be appreciated".

William James

As humans, it is normal to take people and things for granted. It is rarely intentional; however, we are surprised when it is brought to our attention. People are quite wrapped up in their everyday life with family, work etc.

It is a rarity not to hear the words "I just don't have the time", "I can't believe where the time has flown", (as if it actually had wings). People fail to take the time to stop and smell the roses or watch the grass grow. It is polite to say "thank you" to each other wherever you are; in shops, restaurants, social outings and with family and friends. Take a little time and connect to the emotion of gratitude.

Task:
You will need a comfortable chair, a note-book and pen for this exercise

Shake out your body and loosen up

In a seated position allow yourself to ease out and relax

Take a few breaths by inhaling and exhaling deeply

Focus on your breathing as you sense the easy rise and fall of your chest that happens all by itself

Now, in your own mind softly, gently and slowly repeat the words "thank you", about three times.

Imagine the colour of gratitude flowing in and around you, as you repeat the words "thank you"

Notice the feeling that fills you

Open your eyes.

Now, make a list of all the people in your life for whom you are grateful;

....
....
....
....
....

Make a list of what you are grateful for in your life e.g. your life, your body, you're home, possessions etc Include as much detail as possible;

....
....
....
....
....

> *"Gratitude unlocks the fullness of life. It turns what we have into enough, and more. It turns denial into acceptance, chaos into order, confusion into clarity.... It turns problems into gifts, failures into success, the unexpected into perfect timing, and mistakes into important events. Gratitude makes sense of our past, brings peace for today and creates a vision for tomorrow."*
>
> Melodie Beattie

When unhappy with ourselves in the present we have a tendency to view our past with disdain and as unfortunate. The future in turn either cannot exist and/ or seems pretty dull, bleak and depressing. This is a trick of the mind that you can change. This technique is simple and must be practised during your worst moments...

Strategy:
Just affirm three things for which that you are truly grateful;

Example:
I am grateful for my eyes
I am grateful for my hands
I am truly grateful for my legs

Thank you for my home
Thank you for the electricity that works every time
Thank you for my TV

I am truly grateful for the love in my life
I am truly grateful for my health
I am truly grateful for my happy nature

Thank you for my family
Thank you for my friends
Thank you for my education

Then affirm in the present everything that you desire and are grateful for in advance:

Thank you for my ideal job
Thank you for the money I need to buy that house.
Thank you that I passed my exams

I am truly grateful for my new car
I am truly grateful for the career successes in my life
I am truly grateful for the abundance my children experience forever

Thank you for the joy and peace in my life
Thank you for the respect I have for new friends
Thank you for the success of our publications

I am truly grateful for renewed health and vitality

I am truly grateful for my enhanced wisdom
I am truly grateful for being a kinder, more generous, loving and grateful person everyday.

Make a vow to yourself now that, when you awaken each day that before you put your feet on the floor that you affirm:

I am grateful for this wonderful new day.

I am grateful for

....
....
....
....
....

I am grateful for

....
....
....
....
....

"If the only prayer you said in your whole life was, "thank you," that would suffice."

Meister Eckhart

"As we express our gratitude, we must never forget that the highest appreciation is not to utter words, but to live by them."

John F. Kennedy

"Let us rise up and be thankful, for if we didn't learn a lot today, at least we learned a little, and if we didn't learn a little, at least we didn't get sick, and if we got sick, at least we didn't die; so, let us all be thankful."

Budda

"*To speak gratitude is courteous and pleasant, to enact gratitude is generous and noble, but to live gratitude is to touch Heaven.*"

Johannes A. Gaertner

"*Blessed are those that can give without remembering and receive without forgetting.*"

Author Unknown

"*You simply will not be the same person two months from now after consciously giving thanks each day for the abundance that exists in your life. And you will have set in motion an ancient spiritual law: the more you have and are grateful for, the more will be given you.*"

Sarah Ban Breathnach

Simple Abundance

Now close all the windows in your mansion. Draw the curtains and we will see you in the next chapter...

QUESTIONS & ANSWERS
TO BE OR NOT TO BE

This chapter is about common problems that people seek advice on. Some of these problems in the questions below are emotional, psychological and physical. Indeed, some of the problems in the questions below may be familiar to you or to a loved one. All names have been withheld to protect the guilty and to maintain client confidentiality. The clients and the therapists also are fictitious so their confidentiality is moot.

All joking aside enjoy the final chapter in this book and we hope that some of your questions will soon be well answered

When should you call the doctor? Call the doctor when "you're not sure". Many medical centres have an advisory nurse you can call when you are concerned about your health matters. Generally, they are in a position to put your mind at ease or suggest that you see your doctor without delay or go to A&E department pronto. Whatever the problem make sure to call because what might seem like a small matter could be something more serious and what might seem serious could well be a minor issue. In any case, just call, because you are better off safe than sorry!

Dear Dr. Killem Fersher:

I am, generally, a healthy person with two very active children and a moaner of a husband who works extremely long hours. I am a part time teacher. Lately, anyway, I have noticed that I am edgy and nervous. I get panicky at the slightest thing, and regularly get pains in my chest. Could there be something wrong with my heart, as heart problems run in my family? I don't know what to do.. Is this serious, and should I be particularly concerned?

Chesty Paigne

Dear Ms. Paigne:

With your family history it makes sense to have a full check up, including a check for cholesterol, blood sugar and an ECG, to rule out any cardiac problems. However, it is very likely that you are just under a lot of stress at the moment. It might be a good idea to schedule some quality time with your husband. Get a babysitter to look after the kids, at least once a week. It appears that you are both under a lot of stress, and unless you take active steps to counter this, it will only get worse.

Dear Dr. Hag N. Das:

I am pretty sure that I have a gambling problem. I have always enjoyed a flutter on the ponies, and love the social aspects to a good game of poker at the weekends with my friends. Lately though, I feel that I cannot control my gambling. It is no longer just a hobby, but has started to control my life. Yesterday, my friend suggested that I could not control my gambling.. "Bet I can" I replied.

Chas Ino Royale

Dear Mr. Royale:
  It sounds like you do have a gambling problem and it
  is equally probable that you already know this. So the
  question is not "have you got a problem" but rather how
  do we sort the problem out. The first and most important
  step is admitting you have a problem so you are well on
  your way. The next step is to get some support in under-
  standing what the gambling was helping you cope with.
  In other words are there other areas in your life that are
  causing you stress and perhaps now might be a good time
  to find alternative ways to relax and switch off. Consider
  some form of group therapy and take up a non competi-
  tive physical exercise like running or jogging.

Dear Dr. Kill Joy:

  I have been down in the dumps lately as I think that I may
  have inherited a rare blood disease. My grandmother had
  it and it is called pernicious anaemia.

  The doctors can't seem to find anything wrong with me
  and they have done all kinds of tests. But still I feel ill and
  it is affecting my life. I have all the symptoms; the loss of
  breath, run down constantly I can't eat certain foods.
  There is no joy in my life anymore. My question to you is,
  is there anything else that I can do to uncover this disease
  if it is really there or what should I do now?
                                          Desperate Diana

Dear Desperate Diana,
  If your doctors have done the normal range of tests, evi-
  dence of the anaemia should have shown up. It is very
  common to experience the symptoms of an illness, about
  which you are worrying about constantly. Obviously this
  doesn't imply that your feelings are not real – they are
  - to you. We suggest that you might consider getting a

*second or third opinion from another doctor, a special-
ist to put your mind at ease and even visit a reputable
Complimentary Medical Practitioner.
Something else you can do is to imagine how your life
would be if you didn't have this fear. Take some time
and notice what you would focus on instead. In fact just
imagine that you are in your best health and begin to live
your life this way.*

Dear Dr. Happy Tebeheer,

*I am 63 years old and have just lost my job. The company
in question said it was due to down sizing and the down
turn in the economy. I find that hard to believe as my
position was replaced with a younger Harvard guy. My
life is rotten now as my social life was built around my
job. I was in the bowling team, golf club and took part in
mentoring. My income is now halved and my spirits are
low. I noticed that I have been getting pains in my lower
back and knees. I would appreciate any help that you
could give me.
Thanks,*

Too-old-To-die-Young

*Dear Too-Old-To-Die-Young,
That is really tough losing your job like that for whatever
reason. It sounds like your life has turned upside down.
You must begin to focus on turning this situation into a
positive. It is truly the only way! Of course, it is easy to
dwell on what happened and feel very unhappy about it
but, the situation is as it is. You need to set new goals
in your life and this includes your personal, social and
work life. You are still a vital man and can easily take all
your valuable experiences and apply them to a new job.
As you mentioned mentoring, we were wondering if you*

thought about teaching in your local school even if it is voluntary for now.

Update your CV or resume, join a local bowling club and give your old friends a call. You may be surprised at how happy they are to hear from you.

Regarding the pains; visit you local medical practitioner, although the pains could well be related to the stress and worry which you have been experiencing.

Dear Dr. Whipdem Tonsilsout,
I am fed up with the way that I look. I have been struggling with my weight for as long as I can remember. This problem goes way back since I was a child. Although I am fairly confident, I hate my bum because it is too big and my stomach is massive. I am 5ft 2inches and look like a barrel. Is there any hope for me? I must say that I have been thinking of liposuction and a tummy tuck. I wonder will it work, and if it will last. By the way I am pretty inactive and I don't see that changing in the near future.
Sincerely,

Fatty Bum-Bum

Dear Fatty Bum-Bum,
Well the good news is, is that you can do whatever you choose to do, because this is your life and welcome to it! The ideal solution for you is to increase your activity levels and improve your nutritional quality and quantity. You say that you are fairly confident, yet you hate your bum. You need to start liking your bum after all you have been sitting on it for the longest time – almost like a comfy chair wouldn't you say?

Visit your local Medical Practitioner and ask for a referral to a cosmetic surgeon. Ensure that you do your homework by researching all that you can including side ef-

fects from anaesthetic, and when things might go wrong, e.g. clots, super bugs, post operation expectations and infections.

Once you see your surgeon for the initial consult, he should be able to answer specific questions and make sure you listen to him, understand fully and it's a good idea to take notes.

It is also important to get referrals and/or recommendations before choosing a surgeon and surgical procedure. Make sure the doctor is qualified, licensed and (bonded) insured.

Dear Dr. Reisin Temp,
    I have been getting hot flushes and severe bouts of depression lately. I find it hard to sleep which makes me tired during the day. I have thought that it could be my menopause, yet I am only 36 years of age. I haven't been for a full check up because I was hoping that this might be psychological and just go away. I don't know what to think anymore.
Thanks,

Hot Stuff

Dear Hot Stuff:
    Well there could be a range of things going on here, but before we start to make any type of diagnosis, you had better take yourself off to the doctor for a full blood screening. This should include a variety of hormone tests including an oestrogen check.

Regarding menopause; it is not uncommon to have menopausal symptoms at an early age. This is called perimenopause and it is nothing to be concerned about. There are many practical steps that you can take to ease

these symptoms. Take a good look at your lifestyle and introduce some stress management techniques including some gentle exercises like yoga or tai-chi.
Try to wear cotton clothing to help your skin breath better. Avoid deodorants so that your body can perspire naturally. Have some cool showers and cut back on caffeinated and alcohol drinks. Processed foods have been known to affect the body's natural balance, so more natural food products could help also. It is always best to visit a nutritionist as well as your doctor.

Dear Dr. Ark Eology
I am a fossil. I am old and I look old. My face is all crinkled up like an old prune. I have been a sun worshiper all my life and I couldn't imagine wearing a pair of shorts or T-shirt without a great tan. Anyway I am now 55years old and even though I am fabulously tanned I look wretched. If you saw me you would agree.
What can I do to look healthy and youthful again? Needless to say that this is making me depressed. Is there a cosmetic procedure that I can avail of?
Thanks,

Al E. Gator

Dear Al,
It sounds to us that your concerns are more on the psychological side than that of a physical problem.
You have had some wonderful years of looking great and by the sounds of it you have escaped some pretty nasty diseases. So you have lots to be happy about. Now you are moving on in years, and that is great too! Focus on your attributes and other aspects of your life; your achievements, your personality, qualities, family etc.

The other thing that we suggest is that you visit a reputable cosmetic advisor.

You might want to ask yourself "Is Cosmetic Surgery for you"?
As with all plastic surgery, good health and realistic expectations are essential.

What are your goals?

(a) to improve the overall facial appearance
(b) to look ten years younger
(c) Defy the ageing process

Get clear and get real!

Factors that affect the outcome of cosmetic surgery are:

Skin type e.g. oily, dry, combination, skin conditions like acne, ethnic background, elasticity, individual healing, bone structure, as well as practical expectations. All factors should be discussed prior to surgery. Cosmetic procedures are sometimes performed on patients in their thirties, and even as early as twenties. Successful surgery is been performed on patients in their eighties. Some cosmetic surgery is essential due to traffic and work related accidents. Most cosmetic surgery is done, however, on a voluntary basis for reasons of vanity and self-confidence. Cosmetic procedures cannot stop ageing, nor can it turn back the clock. What it can do is help people look their best and give a look of health and a more youthful appearance. A positive side benefit is that many patients' experience increased self-confidence.

There are other non-invasive procedures available such as face fillers. However investigate some of the contributory factors in ageing below and see if you can make some positive changes in your life.

There are many factors that cause ageing besides sun damage and they are:
Heredity, lifestyle choice; alcohol consumption, cigarette smoking, recreational drug use, stress habits, dehydration, depression, illness, fear, unhappiness, poor exercise regime, and a negative and worried attitude to life all contribute to the ageing process.

Ask yourself:

Are you open and honest about your age?

....
....
....
....
....

Are you open and honest about your cosmetic enhancers?

....
....
....
....
....

Do you accept that you physical appearance is changing.

....
....
....
....
....

Always do your research first.
It is vital to focus on your inner-confidence, which is more long lasting.

Dear Dr. Bart Ender

I have been seeing a psychiatrist for alcoholism and I can't seem to kick the habit. I fall off the wagon every couple of months and my life turns to rubbish. I have lost faith in myself, as my wife left me and my kids won't speak to me. Should I just resign myself to drinking for the rest of my life as I actually get great comfort from it. I can't really see my life without it. I am actually pretty lonely.
Thanks,

Jack Daniels

Dear Jack,

It is normal to get 'ants in your pants' during therapy. It often happens that you just don't see the point in continuing because nothing seems to be getting any better. Alcohol is not a friend. Alcohol is a drug and you are hooked on it so you might want to consider your life completely without it. If you had an infectious tumour that was affecting your entire body wouldn't you want to remove it completely? The same thing applies to drug abuse – alcoholism.

As long as you are relaxed about falling off the wagon, as if it is some western movie that you are starring in, you won't get to the next stage.
We are wondering if you considered some group therapy, along with the 'one-on-one' therapy you are doing with your shrink. This could help provide greater interaction and objective feed back.

It sounds like you have been working on the reasons you drink. It may be time now to focus on the reasons to stop. You need to spend time on planning your future. Create a compelling future; Believe, behave and become.

Dear Dr. Savin L. Ives,
  Everyone is telling me that I look terrible. They are mak-
  ing me crazy. Although I have been in a few car wrecks
  and have suffered with my general health and nerves, I
  feel overwhelmed by other peoples concerns. Ok, so I
  know that I don' eat that well and my lifestyle is pretty
  poor. Perhaps you can give me some hints on how to re-
  store my health and general well-being.
  Ta,

  Need-a-make-over

Dear Need-a-make-over,
  Listen to your own intuition and don't ask others to diagnose you. You ultimately know how your own health
  and well being is. Signs are what are obvious to you and
  others. Symptoms are the feelings you get. For instance if
  you begin to feel unusually tired, lack lustre with loss of
  joie-de-vivre, these are your *symptoms.*

  Some general hints for you:
  Be mindful of shortness of breath and sudden weight loss
  etc. Pay attention to any unusual signs or symptoms that
  may occur or are recurring. Take note if others notice a
  change in your temperament and attitude.

  Good friends should always let you know.
  It's important not to diagnose yourself. You may well be
  right, but you are not objective. The function of a qualified physician is to assess, determine and diagnose; to advise and help people towards improved health and to tell
  you the truth, even when you don't want to hear it.

  The sooner you seek medical advice the faster a diagnosis
  is reached. Prevention from further complications can be
  achieved and in this case don't put off until tomorrow
  that which you can do today.

Dear Dr. Breakem N. Fixum,
People just walk all over me. I can never seem to get what
I want or even say what I want to say. Every time I try to
say how I feel I get tongue tied and end up saying nothing
and just going with the crowd. I just feel so angry inside
and swear each time that I will stick up for myself. It
never happens though. How can I express myself without
going crazy?

Going Crazy Girl

Response:

Dear Going Crazy Girl,
First of all this is easier than you think. Good news be-
cause you are aware of what you are doing and not doing.
All you need to know now is what you need to be doing
and how to do it. Right now say how you feel: I feel a
bit overwhelmed right now... I'd like to offer my opinion
about this. State what it is.
Simply practice what you want to say, know when you
intend to say it and most importantly take a few cleans-
ing breaths and go for it.
Throw in the odd smile as it helps you relax and has a
good affect on those whom you are speaking to.

Section 10

CONCLUSIONS
AND AFTERTHOUGHTS....

Way back there on the first page of this book we laid out our aims...

We wanted this book to help you make the right lifestyle-choices to remain healthy for as long as possible; to recover from ill health when it happens; and to live with ill health in a positive way when recovery is not possible.

We broadly looked at health under the two sections – Physical, and Emotional/Mental health. We tried to show how easy it is to let yourself slip from a healthy state into an unhealthy state, and when in that unhealthy state, how easy it is to maintain the lifestyle habits that keep you in that unhealthy state.

We have tried to show you a number of techniques, some orthodox, some unorthodox, that will help you break the patterns that are stopping you from becoming healthy (or at least becoming as healthy as possible). Not all of these techniques will work for you. Some will be completely unsuitable. But some will, and you may find that you will develop your own techniques that build on these.

We have discussed, using case histories, the effects of life style on physical health. We showed that there is a cause-and-effect dynamic in our physical health, and that we can use that dynamic to break the unhealthy patterns in our behaviour. We discussed both conventional and alternative/complementary therapies. We also showed that your physical health effects your emotional/mental health, and vice versa. When thinking about health, it is important to think *holistically*. We are extremely complex multisystem organisms. We live in an even more complex environment or ecosystem. Trying to treat any one aspect of our organism in isolation is rarely likely to bring about a good result.

We spent some time on emotions, both negative and positive. Emotions provide feedback on our behaviour. Emotions directly affect our behaviour. Emotions directly affect our physical health, as our physical health affects our emotions. We discussed our major emotional states, happiness, love, compassion and forgiveness.

We felt it was important to take an in depth consideration of Carolyn Myss' concept of *Archetypes*. Archetypes are essentially neutral but have both *shadow* and *light* aspects. We pointed out that these should not necessarily be considered "good" and "bad", but as different aspects of the same archetype. We discussed the four main archetypes, the *victim*, the *saboteur*, the *prostitute*, and the *child*. We then examined a few or our favourite archetypes in more detail. We suggested that you look at the archetypes that apply to you, and even to come up with some archetypes of your own. Then see how these illuminate your own personality.

These concepts form the building blocks that this book is built on.

Relationships are the infrastructure on which our lives are constructed. While it is easy to concentrate on romantic or love relationships, it is important to remember that every interaction we have with our environment is a relationship. It is important to remember that we have relationships at work, at play, with our friends, family and even with "things" and pets.

In our discussion of emotional health, we have not only focused on positive emotions, but we have also considered negative emotions – anger; fear; depression; hatred; guilt. These emotions are not always negative. We briefly talked about "thinking too much" and obsessing on what we feel is negative. We suggested ways to turn "negative" emotions around so that positive results are achieved in a realistic way, for you.

We looked at the role of music in our lives, how it affects both our emotional and physical health. There are many interesting ways that music has been used to improve health. Some of these techniques form the basis of music therapies, which are gaining popularity in recent years.

We used the imaginary concept of a mansion with many windows as an interesting way to look at all the issues brought up in the book so far. It is one method of looking at health *holistically*. It is also an attempt to think positively about our circumstances. Using a metaphor of a mansion with many windows, we can see all the things that we should be grateful for. Each window gives us a different world view. Some of these views are quite depressing, but we can learn from what we see, and apply it to our own world. This is an excellent model showing how we can use metaphors as a way of seeing our problems in an objective rather than subjective way. We get lost in negatively perceived self realisations because we are unable to view our circumstances objectively.

In summary, your health cannot be isolated to a small aspect of your life. Your health is your life, and every aspect impacts on every other aspect. Your emotional health impacts on your physical health. Your surroundings, both psychological and physical, impact on your physical and emotional health. Any improvement in one aspect of your health and circumstances, improves all other aspects. Any deleterious impact affects all other aspects.

This book is not intended as the answer to all your health problems. Medical Doctors spend their entire lives studying, and still do not have the answer to all health problems. What we have done in a single volume, is introduce you to a number of ideas, and approaches. We hope that you will then feel motivated to look further, and to try your own approaches. Remember, nothing succeeds like success. If you set a reasonable target, and achieve it, you will feel motivated to enjoy unleashing even further achievements resulting in greater happiness. Anything is achievable with the right motivation, but getting motivated is the hard part.

What will work for one person; will not necessarily work for another. Everyone has to find their own healthy lifestyle, and there are many compromises that may have to be made. This is not necessarily a bad thing. It is better to make a small improvement that you are likely to maintain, than make a severe change that you will stop after a few days.

"I spent a fortune on that gymnasium and didn't lose a pound... Turns out they expected me to turn up!" Anonymous

At the end of the day, there is nothing magical or complicated about looking after your health. A common sense approach will never fail you. Always ask yourself "Does this make sense?" If it does it is probably correct.

Final Quote:

> *"Anyone who goes to see a psychiatrist should have his head examined."*
>
> Samuel L. Goldwyn

RECOMMENDED READING

General

Bandler Richard, *Get the Life that you Want*, London: Harper Collins, 2008

Borysenko, Joan Z, *Fried*, USA: Hay House, 2011

Breslin, Murphy, *Your Life only a Gazillion Times Better*, London: Random House, 2006

Mc Kenna, Paul, *Change your Life in 7 Days*, London: Bantam Press, 2004

Neill, Michael, *Super Coach*, USA: Hay House 2010

Physical Health

Myss, Caroline, Shealy, Norman C, *The Creation of Health*, New York: Three River Press, 1998

Northrup, Dr. Christiane, *Womens Bodies, Womens Wisdom*, USA: Random House, 2010

Williamson, Marianne, *A Course in Weight Loss*, USA: Hay House Inc., 2010

Emotional Health

Holden, Robert, *Happiness Now*, USA: Hay House, Inc. 2007

Myss, Caroline, *Why People don't Heal and How they Can*, Great Britain: Bantam House 1998

Ohotto, Robert, *Transforming Fate into Destiny*, USA: Hay House, 2008

Vanzant, Iyanla, *One Day My Soul Just Opened Up*, Great Britain: Pocket Books, 2002

Archetypes

Myss, Caroline, *Sacred Contracts*, New York, Three River Press, 2002

Relationships

Burns, Dr. David, *Feeling Good Together*, UK: Vermillion, 2009
Kearns, JM, *Better Love Next Time*, UK: Vermillion, 2009
Ruiz, Don Miguel, *The Mastery of Love*, USA: Amber Allen 2002

Music

Aldridge, David, *Music Therapy in Dementia Care*, London: Jessica Kingsley Publishers, 2000
Pavlicevic, Mercédés, *Music Therapy*, London: Jessica Kingsley Publishers, 1999
Wigman, Tony, Pedersey, Nyyaard Inge, & Bonde, Ole Lars *Comprehensive Guide to Music Therapy*, London: Jessica Kingsley Publishers, 2002

Gratitude

Harrell, Keith, *An Attitude of Gratitude*, USA: Hay House, 2004
Hay, Louise L, *Gratitude*, USA: Hay House 1996
Weissman, Dr. Darren, *The Power of Infinite Love and Gratitude*, USA: Hay House 2007